THE SECRET
TRIANGLE

THE SECRET TRIANGLE

Of Life, Death, and Evolution

Rebecca Lynne

BALBOA.
PRESS
A DIVISION OF HAY HOUSE

ISBN: 978-1-4525-3964-5 (sc)
ISBN: 978-1-4525-3819-8 (e)

Balboa Press books may be ordered through booksellers or by contacting:

Balboa Press
A Division of Hay House
1663 Liberty Drive
Bloomington, IN 47403
www.balboapress.com
1-(877) 407-4847

Because of the dynamic nature of the Internet, any web addresses or links contained in
this book may have changed since publication and may no longer be valid. The views
expressed in this work are solely those of the author and do not necessarily reflect the
views of the publisher, and the publisher hereby disclaims any responsibility for them.

The author of this book does not dispense medical advice or prescribe the use of any
technique as a form of treatment for physical, emotional, or medical problems without the
advice of a physician, either directly or indirectly. The intent of the author is only to offer
information of a general nature to help you in your quest for emotional and spiritual well-
being. In the event you use any of the information in this book for yourself, which is your
constitutional right, the author and the publisher assume no responsibility for your actions.

Any people depicted in stock imagery provided by Thinkstock are models,
and such images are being used for illustrative purposes only.
Certain stock imagery © Thinkstock.

Printed in the United States of America

Balboa Press rev. date: 10/12/2011

For All Truth students of past, present,
And future

"Living in the world without becoming aware of the meaning of the world is like wondering about in a great library without ever touching the books."—Manley Hall

Table of Contents

ILLUSTRATIONS WITH COMMENTS

Acknowledgements

Heartfelt thanks to all my students who over the years have wanted to know the "why" of things and inspired me to help them find the answers. They are the ones who dare to believe that our destiny toward total freedom is even now, day by day, being fulfilled. Because a teacher learns by teaching, they have helped me along the way.

I would like to acknowledge the Unity Movement in which I received Ordination and have worked so happily. Unity's books written by its Founder, Charles Fillmore, were discovered soon after my initial awakening to spiritual insight. These have been invaluable to me in the study and teaching of Truth principles.

Appreciation goes to Rebecca Blowers for her fine work in illustrating these abstract ideas. Only a good Truth student, who was willing to put in many long hours discussing interpretation of Creation's universal laws could have drawn them with such understanding and clarity.

Without the help and guidance of my wonderful daughter, Kriste Lindenmeyer, I would not have been able to work my way through the maze of computer rules. Her constant support and interest in my projects has always been there when I needed expert advice.

To the many others, too numerous to name, I am deeply grateful for their help in presenting this book.

A Special Acknowledgement

TO A SPECIAL FRIEND

In efforts to bring my work to others, I have been blessed with a special friend. He is Dave Mann, who with his tireless work and cheerful attitude has given me invaluable help. He has assisted me in presenting Power Point Workshops, with photography, and with setting up my new Website. He seems to know what I need without being asked and his know-how never fails. I want to acknowledge his outstanding willingness to devote time and encouragement to my projects.

Dave is a physicist and a delightful friend for discussion. His interest in Truth teaching is boundless. He was the chief physicist at Hewlett Packard before retiring. Dave has also been devoted to the study of astronomy since childhood. He is a busy fellow and continues to work by helping others. He is a blessing to everyone who is privileged to know him. Thank you my friend and may your days be filled with Spiritual delight and enlightenment!

Preface

We all have the same questions, no matter where we live, how we live, or how long we live. The questions are within us from the moment we take our first breath, even though we don't recognize them consciously. Actually, they become the dominating force that lies behind everything we experience. The questions push us to experience and experiment with life as it takes us through many twists and turns. Gradually we become more aware of those questions and realize that we must find the answers to them because they demand an answer. You know them, WHO AM I? WHAT AM I? WHY AM I? WHAT WILL HAPPEN TO ME AFTER I DIE? WHY DO I HAVE TO DIE?

The greatest mystery of all, that of life and death, seems so complicated, so convoluted, so multi-layered, that the truth of it will never be known. It is my hope that you, like me, will find the answers to all your questions in the SECRET OF THE TRIANGLE. Once the TRIANGLE is understood, it can become the pathway to full illumination. This book is written to explain that TRIANGLE, where it is to be found, how it has been used, and how we are destined to use it.

I know that you would not have opened this book without having reached a point in your life that prods you to find answers to your questions. To find those answers, you are required to give up old ways of thinking. Knowing the SECRET OF THE TRIANGLE is valuable, but what you are to do with it, requires constant vigilance and an awareness of how to properly utilize its power every day. This takes some time and practice and does not happen without effort.

In your search for truth of Being, no doubt it will eventually become apparent that something is keeping you from embracing it totally. There is a natural human fear of the unknown. As you proceed in your search, your fear will gradually diminish and one day will disappear altogether. You may feel that you are not fearful of knowing the Truth of Who,

What and Why you are, but ask yourself this question, "What is it that I would not want to give up?" Your mind will most likely turn to the "things" of the world or to the love received from family, friends, or perhaps your accomplishments, etc. I would suggest that none of these are what you cherish the most and what you cling to more than anything else.

Your most precious possession is your own identity! Your human identity as a person is important to you because you build your existence around it. It seems to be who you are, but is that true? Knowing how the TRIANGLE works, will eventually cause us to take on a new Identity without fear of losing anything. However, we must trust enough in the unknown to begin taking the necessary steps. This is, at first, an intellectual knowing, then it becomes a heartfelt emotion, and finally we are able to accept the fulfillment we have been seeking.

This cannot be explained quickly or easily. It is a science that must be learned step by step. These pages tell of my own quest for the answer to the mystery of life and death and the destiny of humanity, which led to my realization of the SECRET. I am still working at it and new realizations keep coming. I know there is no end to Truth and that is what brings joy to living. Learning and becoming is the joy of life!

I have inserted some of my personal experiences to illustrate how the SECRET OF THE TRIANGLE has worked in my life. For over forty years I have been teaching this because it is so logical and it is also scientific. Great joy comes in sharing every facet of this insight and it continues to reveal itself to me. Repetition is a marvelous way to learn, so the teacher continues to learn. It is the teacher's hope that the student will also become a teacher and lead others to the rainbow and beyond, where lies the pot of gold we have often seen pictured. What is that gold? Pure gold is the golden Light of God.

Chapter 1

WHAT IS IT ALL ABOUT?

History illustrates that humanity has continually expanded its awareness of something we call God. From the primitive worship of many gods there has been a progressive change of viewpoint. There is every reason to believe that what still remains unknown about God is moment by moment being realized by any number of individuals, worldwide. Church doctrine traditionally has stifled independent thinking and it has been generally accepted that those, other than the Clergy, could not experience significant Spiritual revelation.

Today, those who study sacred scriptures, legends, myths, ancient wisdom teachings and scientific theories are finding that these all reveal similar deep Truths. Combining these esoteric insights is a tremendous help in finding Reality. However, it becomes apparent that nothing is what it appears to be. There is more to everything we think we know because the meaning of what it is all about is cloaked in forms and symbols.

Shall the Truth always be hidden from us? This book is written for those who dare to believe that the door is wide open for us to discover what it is all about. Science today tells us that everything is vibrating energy. As astonishing at it may seem, the Bible tells us the same thing. Science of today is affirming the universal laws of the Bible and how grand it is to know the Truth has always been available.

The story that unfolds here is my own, but it is also YOUR story and the story of all humanity. It is the story of what we call God, as far as we individually, are able to discern it at our present state of evolution.

MY STORY BEGINS

I was nine years old when I was told a secret. It was a secret about life and death. It happened when my Grandmother died. It was in the 1930's during the great depression and my parents didn't have much money. I suppose we were able to make the train-trip from Cincinnati to the little country town in Arkansas because my Aunt's husband worked for the railroad and was able to get free passes. We needed to make the trip because my Grandmother was ill and was not expected to live. Mother wanted to see her beloved Momma again before she died and it was important to her that her two girls would be able to remember their Grandmother.

Mother and Daddy had moved north soon after they married and I had only seen my grandparents one other time. My Grandfather used to be the town Sherriff and now he was Commissioner of the Waterworks. Everyone knew him and called him Uncle Joe. We called him Daddy Joe. The home where Mother grew up was familiar to me. I remembered their big house with shade trees and a wrap-around porch on the front and side. There was a screened-in porch on the back. In the backyard chickens were free to roam and what fun it was to go into the hen house and find eggs in their nests. Living in the city never offered that kind of experience. There is still an unpleasant memory though, that of Daddy Joe wringing the head off a chicken so we could have it for dinner.

There was a huge stove in the kitchen that had a warmer oven above the burners. Here we could always find homemade biscuits or pie. That may be why these are still favorites of mine. There was a big pantry too, big enough to walk into and it was full to the brim. I remember spending time exploring that pantry and enjoying the aroma of good things to eat.

Mother told us how she used to have to take meals over to the jailhouse to feed the prisoners and how it was her job to do the washing in the big metal tubs in the backyard every Tuesday morning before going to school. She had five sisters and three brothers so some of her sisters also took their turn at the washing on other days. The boys had chores too. They were a happy family and I felt that happiness. I had memories full of warm breezes, wonderful aromas from the kitchen, squeaky screen doors and quiet, restful days at that grand place.

This time things were different. Mother and Daddy thought I was old enough to be told about death and to go into the room where Grandmother lay on her bed near death. The family, aunts, uncles, and cousins were there too. Everyone was very solemn and quiet. It was not a happy scene until Grandmother began telling us how her son John, who had been killed in World War I, had come to her, along with his brother Jesse, who had died when still a very young man. She said, "They stood at the foot of the bed and said they were waiting for me. They are going to be with me when I come over." She smiled and seemed to be content. She died the next day and the family talked about how good it was that she was with John and Jesse.

This was my first encounter with death and it was more puzzling to me than it was sad. Did an unseen place exist where John and Jesse were still alive? Was it somehow attached to the place where we lived? How could this be? Was there another place where people were still alive and we could not see them? If so, what was this thing called death? What was it all about? Why would God have bothered to make us and then let us die after all His trouble? It seemed such a dumb thing to do! God should be a lot smarter than that! To me it seemed there was something very wrong about death.

Then I heard a quiet but firm voice. It was inside of me but it didn't feel like it was me. It said, "People are not supposed to die, it is not God's way." I didn't question it or even wonder what I was supposed to do with this information. In childlike innocence it was accepted as true and I felt better. I don't remember wondering about it, or ever sharing this experience with anyone else as I grew into adulthood. It was my secret to keep even if the rest of the world didn't know it. Twenty-nine years would pass before I discovered why we are not supposed to die and this book is an effort to help you make the same discovery.

Do you remember when you first heard about God? I certainly don't. I suppose God is introduced to us so early in our childhood that God just "is." We can choose to believe in a God or not to believe if that makes us more comfortable. My parents didn't go to church but they were believers who told us about God, the Bible, and its teachings.

As a child, one of my favorite pastimes was looking at the beautiful colored pictures of famous paintings in our family Bible. They took me into another world that was mysterious and I wanted to learn more about it. I was eight years old and my sister ten, when a friend of my Mother took us to a Christian Science Church Sunday school. We really liked it, but we moved away soon after that and would not attend another Church until we were teenagers. As teenagers we were old enough to ride the streetcar to Church. We always loved everything about Church, even the Sermons. We attended Sunday school class before the Service and then Young Peoples meeting on Sunday evenings. It was in that Presbyterian congregation that I met and later married my husband.

After five years of marriage, we built a home and started attending a Methodist Church in our new neighborhood. It was in this environment that our two children grew up and where I taught Sunday school, Bible School, sang in the Choir, worked in the Women's Society and served as a Spiritual Leader. Little did I know during those years, that I would become a Minister! I didn't see that in my future. There was only one thing wrong. I knew there must be more to Christianity than I was hearing from the pulpit. Too many of my questions were not being answered. Too often, after the Sermon, I found myself asking, "Why can't the Minister go further, go on, go on! There is more to it than that! There must be explanations for things in the Bible that the Church is not telling us."

Nevertheless, a deep faith in God was embedded within me, which I trusted. At thirty-seven years old something happened that gave me an opportunity to use and deepen that trust. I was seriously injured in a car accident. We were driving to Florida but had decided to visit Washington D.C. on the way. This took us through the mountainous area of Virginia. It was the month of March but still cold and we were caught in an ice storm. My husband had slowed our speed to only forty-five miles an hour because the road was treacherous. Suddenly I heard him say, "We're not going to make this curve!"

The next thing I remember was lying on a stretcher and shaking all over. Someone said, "She is going into shock, get another blanket." After that, I had no conscious awareness until I awoke in the emergency room of a hospital in Winchester, Virginia. They were cutting off my bloody clothes and reassuring me that I was going to be all right.

I didn't know it then, but our car had crashed into a culvert and I had crashed into the dashboard. This was years before cars had shoulder strap seat belts. However, they told me my life was saved by the lap seat belt I was wearing at the time. Thankfully, my husband only suffered two broken ribs and the children had come through with just minor cuts and bruises. My husband told me later that when he looked at me, he saw that my nose had relocated to the right side of my face and the left side had been crushed. I soon became aware that all my front teeth had been broken and that I had a broken collarbone. There was tremendous pain in my back so I knew I was in serious condition.

The most amazing thing about this event in my life was that it became a spiritual awakening for me. While lying on a gurney in the hall, while they prepared a room for me, I felt no fear or anxiety, but was sure that God was with me. I remember saying, "God I know you are with me, just hold my hand." At that moment I actually felt another hand clasped with mine. There was pain but that didn't matter, I knew I would be healed. From that moment, something I had never experienced before enveloped me night and day. It was as though I was floating within a soft cloud of love.

My doctors worked wonders and I loved them and all the nurses too. They put my nose back where it belonged and I was wrapped in bandages. Ministers and Priests from the town came to visit and pray with me. Loving Get Well cards came from friends at home and my Minister sent me a card every day. It is something difficult to put into words, but there was this continuous day-by-day sense of floating in love. I didn't know it then, but have come realize that I was experiencing a taste of the Spiritual Love that permeates the atmosphere of a higher dimension.

My lips were so swollen that I could see them extending out below my nose. I could only drink through a straw at first, but gradually the swelling went down and the doctors did some more work on my nose. After that first day I experienced no more back pain. The plan was to put me in a cast from my neck to my hips when the swelling subsided so that my back could heal. After two weeks in the hospital they took new x-rays in preparation for the cast and were astonished to find no evidence of the injuries they had seen before. I knew God's love had healed my back.

After returning home, I gradually resumed my life with my arm in a cast to heal the collarbone. The healing process for my face required more plastic surgery. My plastic surgeon marveled at the good job the doctors had done. I had to replace lost teeth and after months of healing I looked just about the same as before the accident. There was no doubt however, that the accident had been a blessing in disguise because it served as a leap into a Spiritual world that was new to me. I now enjoyed an unshakeable faith in an **invisible Presence** that was always with me. In retrospect, it is clear that this was a higher and yet deeper foundation of faith that would serve to lead me into tremendous changes in my life.

About a year later, I was suddenly very troubled about a statement made by Jesus. It was in the book of Mathew, Chapter 5:48 *"Be ye perfect as your Father in Heaven is already perfect."* I wondered why Jesus would expect us to be as perfect as God. We were only human beings! I went to my Minister about my concern. After all, if I could not accept this statement, how then, could I continue to believe in anything that Jesus taught? The Minister answered, "When we die and go to Heaven we will know what Jesus meant."

It was clear to me that he didn't know the secret about life and death, so I was not satisfied with his answer. Shortly after this, a new Minister was assigned to our Church and I discussed this same Scripture passage with him. He told me that certain secrets were kept from us because we were not yet ready to understand them. This made more sense to me but I was not willing to accept that we could not find the answers to all our questions here and now.

I heard that some people had read the Bible all the way through and I decided this was the way to find out what I wanted to know. Surely, the answer to this question and many others must be in there somewhere, just waiting for me to read them. One evening after the children had gone to bed and my husband was watching television, I went into the bedroom, settled in a comfy chair, and began to read the Creation Story in the Book of Genesis. I finished the first chapter and half of the next one, when an inner voice spoke, "You don't understand what you are reading."

I immediately started over again, this time reading more slowly and trying to see more than I had before. Nothing seemed different that evening. It was several days before I was able to read again and this time I went through three chapters but the voice came again, "You don't understand what you are reading, go back." With a sigh, I obeyed and still nothing was revealed. To me, it seemed a story of creation that anyone could understand.

About two weeks passed, but my reading never covered more than the first five chapters of Genesis. Then one evening, again the voice spoke, but this time it was very demanding, "Go back to the beginning!" In my frustration, I spoke aloud, "I have gone back to the beginning!" When I heard the word "beginning" spoken aloud it was as though a veil dropped from my eyes and I saw the word "beginning" in the first sentence of the Bible as a symbol.

A door had been opened and I was then able to see more words as symbols for their real meaning. Gradually, word after word, night after night, I saw the whole of God's Plan, the whole fantastic and magnificent scheme of Creation. A door in my mind had opened to reveal the laws that govern our Solar System, our Cosmos, and our individual souls. The unveiling of these words linked me with a new kind of God, all of Creation, and every other soul in our Universe.

I want to share the reading of Genesis with you now in the hope that it will do the same for you. We will look closely at the words of Genesis, but before we do, I want you to recall the discovery of Einstein.

Einstein's discovery of $E=MC^2$ showed that light, mass, and energy are all connected. Indeed, they are all one in different forms of expression. Science explains that electric energy engages with inert matter and that the velocity of vibration in the mass can be speeded up to reach the speed of light with the result being that mass can be converted to light. Conversely, light can be converted to mass. The creation story of Genesis, in coded symbolic language, tells the same story. It shows how energy engages in seven stages to ultimately take form as matter, time, and space. Einstein talked about the action of radiation and magnetism. He explained how mass attracts light to produce form. This is exactly what Genesis shows us.

After we see what God **really** created, I will tell you more of my personal story. Now let's look inside the symbolic words of Genesis, just as I did many years ago. They are always with me, directing my life.

They are an infallible yardstick to measure the false from the true.

They are a guide to solving any problem.

How much do you want to know?

If you are ready to leave your old ideas behind and begin anew, then read on.

Chapter 2

SEEING WORDS AS SYMBOLS

There really are no secrets concerning life but truth remains a mystery and lies hidden until we become intellectually curious about the plan and purpose of life. The symbols in the Bible can be understood by any of us who are willing to stretch our thinking beyond present limits. To unravel the truth of the scriptures we must also have a fervent heart's desire to know the truth. We must want to know more than the history the Bible records, more than the moral codes of conduct it teaches and more than the religious practice it recommends. It is also necessary that we be ready to sacrifice our traditional interpretations and to see ourselves in an entirely new way. If we have a genuine desire for truth and a willingness to risk losing what we already believe about ourselves and God, the first few chapters in Genesis may reveal some of the secrets to us.

Actually, all the Truth about us, God, Christ, God's Plan, universal laws, and the universe itself are written into this one brief section of the Bible. The "Truth that can set us free" of which Jesus Christ spoke, is cloaked in symbols. This section of the Bible is multi-layered and covers every aspect of creation from the atom to the Cosmos. Its laws reign supreme in every level of experience, both in the visible and invisible realms. These first few chapters of the Bible are a composite of all the Truth contained in the rest of its pages. Thoroughly understood, all the Genesis stories are capable of totally transforming the outlook of the reader. With this in mind we can read parts of this astonishing collection of Truths, expecting some degree of personal transformation. It all begins here.

GENESIS 1

IN THE BEGINNING

We must start from the premise that there is a new way to see these words, a way that we have not yet discovered. Let's assume that we do not understand what they mean. Asking questions brings answers. Let's try it . . .

What is the BEGINNING?

Where is the BEGINNING?

How does it relate to us and how can we know it?

Where does everything begin for us? Possibly, the following could be the correct answers to these questions:

The BEGINNING is mind.

Mind is everywhere. Everything is related to us through our mind and we cannot know anything except through mind. With observation it is easy to see that mind is the BEGINNING for everything in our experience. We cannot be aware of, or experience anything except through mental recognition. Let us then assume that the writer of Genesis is using the BEGINNING as a symbol for mind. If we proceed with this premise, we can read the first words in the Bible like this:

IN THE MIND

Where is MIND?
Since we cannot experience any condition without being conscious of it, MIND is present wherever we are. MIND is everywhere present. There is no escape from MIND. It is omnipresent.
The generally accepted belief is that every person has a mind of

their own and that each person's mind is separate from everyone else's. However, according to these first words in the Bible, this belief simply cannot be true! More than one mind is not mentioned. The word is not BEGINNINGS, but BEGINNING. One MIND is everywhere present and everyone uses the One MIND. Therefore, we must conclude that everyone has consciousness in this One MIND.

All people are in the same BEGINNING and share the same MIND.

This realization defies any concept of self that claims a separate identity. Through invisible MIND, or consciousness, we are linked with all others and all things, even while we feel separate from everyone and everything. This is an important Truth, for herein lies a paradox. We are individual, and yet, we are one with all others and everything that exists, even the Cosmos. Indeed, the ability to be aware of our individuality and at the same time to be aware of the oneness of MIND is essential to spiritual illumination and much effort will be spent in this book to explain this oneness and paradoxical duality.

Let's also realize that we are not talking about the brain of a human being. The brain is a portion of the vertebrate central nervous system in the physical body. It is the organ of thought and neural coordination and receives stimuli from the sense organs. In this first line of the Bible, a physical brain does not exist. MIND is the organized conscious and unconscious adaptive mental activity of an organism. It is esoteric, in the sense that it is not obvious but is hidden. The brain is the exoteric, or the obvious physical receiver and transmitter for the esoteric MIND. To put it simply, shall we say that one is the inner and the other the outer?

IN THE BEGINNING GOD

Where is GOD?

We have established that BEGINNING is MIND. This passage states that GOD is in the BEGINNING, therefore, GOD is in MIND. If MIND is where we are, then GOD is where we are. Therefore,

GOD is with us in MIND. If we choose to believe this, it follows that we must let go of any belief that we are separate from GOD and realize that any separation from GOD can only be in consciousness. According to the first words of the Bible, we are one with GOD through mental recognition. We are consciously linked with GOD by our own thinking.

IN THE BEGINNING, GOD CREATED

These words establish that GOD does the work of creation in MIND! This is a fundamental truth we must grasp in order to get a new perspective about GOD. The Bible states that GOD CREATED in MIND; therefore, MIND is the workshop where creation takes place. We can prove this right now by creating something in MIND. Since MIND is everywhere present we don't have to go anywhere to create. We live in MIND now. As an experiment, think of a snow covered mountain. Now, can you see it? You have created it in MIND. This proves that we can create in MIND and Genesis will show us how this imaging power causes creation.

[See Figure 1]
[See Figure 2]

Figure #1

IN THE BEGINNING

Now let's create an image of MIND itself. This is a little difficult since we have never seen MIND. How shall we do it? Let's think blank or black, the way MIND appears in illustration #1. This is blankness because MIND is invisible and is represented by black to indicate the invisible source of all things . . . MIND!

Figure #2

IN THE BEGINNING GOD

Since the Bible says that GOD is IN THE BEGINNING, we have to place GOD in MIND. It seems laughable for us to picture GOD, but let's settle for a point of light to represent GOD.

If we want to get at the Truth, we must now ask ourselves the **BIG** question.

What is GOD?

The Bible does not say, but it does tell us in its very first line that GOD'S nature is to CREATE. Let's think about that for a moment. We will have to compare GOD to something that is creative in order to better understand the creative nature of GOD. What else is creative? How about a seed? A seed is creative because it produces something out of itself. It is a unit of energy that produces. Is God a unit of creative energy that produces? Since there are many places in the Bible where seeds are used to illustrate a point of creativity let's continue to utilize this idea as our model. Science tells us that energy vibrates, forming patterns, so let's see energy vibrating and moving in the seed.

[See Figure 3]

Figure #3

IN THE MIND GOD SEED

We can now alter our representative image of GOD just a bit. We can image GOD as a seed with innate properties. This seed symbolizes GOD as a unit of vibrating creative energy. From this point on we shall assume that the nature of GOD is comparable to a seed.

Now let's finish reading the first line of the Bible.

IN THE BEGINNING, GOD CREATED HEAVEN AND EARTH

Comparing the GOD SEED to any seed that has been planted, we know it will sprout roots. The GOD SEED is in the soil of MIND and once planted CREATES two roots out of Itself. These two roots are called HEAVEN AND EARTH.

Let's pretend we don't know anything about HEAVEN AND EARTH. What could they be? Since everything is taking place in MIND, we need to know what is in MIND. Ideas are in MIND. Is HEAVEN an idea? Is EARTH an idea? If so, what is the nature of these two ideas? To answer this, we must explore the nature of a seed. A seed has two properties within it which we shall name life and substance. If GOD, a unit of vibrating energy, is a seed, these two ideas are the properties of that seed. They correspond to the life and substance that we find in all seeds. Now we have it:

HEAVEN is an idea of Life
EARTH is an idea of Substance.

Both these ideas can be described as vibrating electrical energy. They exist in MIND!

[See Figure 4]

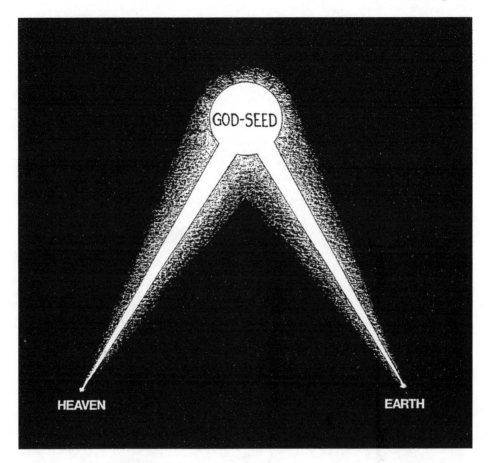

Figure #4

GOD CREATED HEAVEN AND EARTH

We have decided that HEAVEN is an idea of vibrating Life in MIND and EARTH is the idea of vibrating Substance in MIND. GOD was acting as one force, but now we have GOD acting as a threefold force of vibrating energy. Everything else that transpires in MIND will stem from this trinity.

The GOD SEED has become a threefold Principle of creative energy. The nature of this Principle is crucial to our understanding of Truth because it is the TRIANGLE of all creation. It is the governor of involution, evolution, life and death. Through the operating forces of this TRIANGLE the mysteries of our existence can be solved.

AND THE EARTH WAS WITHOUT FORM AND VOID

Since EARTH is an idea, it is easy to understand this phrase. Does an idea in your MIND have tangible form? No! This idea of Substance (EARTH) has no form so it is described as VOID, meaning it is a vacuum. We must be careful here and not think of this EARTH as soil or as the planet Earth. The Bible is talking about the nature of Substance in the Absolute realm of Being (verb). In the creative MIND it is VOID, which indicates that it has a capacity to draw something into itself. Substance is a vacuum waiting to be filled.

AND DARKNESS WAS UPON THE FACE OF THE DEEP

In this passage, that which was called VOID is further described as DEEP, thereby indicating again its capacity to receive. What is there to be received? Since all this happens in MIND and involves only the two ideas that have been CREATED in MIND, it must mean that the EARTH idea is going to receive the HEAVEN idea. The conclusion must be drawn that EARTH has the ability to receive HEAVEN!

Keep this in MIND because herein lies the purpose our lives and the inner message of the Bible. This capacity for union between HEAVEN and EARTH is an important key to unlocking the mystery of human existence. HEAVEN and EARTH are meant to be one, and as this symbolic story unfolds, we shall see that the penetration of HEAVEN into EARTH will happen in gradual stages over long periods of time.

In order to more clearly understand this Bible passage let's analyze the word HEAVEN. We have already established that it is an idea and ideas are often described as intelligence or light. Now we can see why this passage says there was DARKNESS UPON THE FACE OF THE DEEP. DARKNESS is the opposite of light. The light idea of HEAVEN can penetrate into the DARKNESS (VOID) since it is a vacuum. The scripture is telling us that the intelligence of GOD at the Absolute level is radiant Light which will enter into the DARKNESS, the magnetic vacuum of Substance.

The word FACE gives us another clue. FACE indicates "sur-face," which also means "capacity to recognize." Since all this is happening in MIND, we must conclude there is a "capacity to recognize" the radiant idea when it is drawn into magnetic Substance. Aha! Divine Intelligence (ideas) can penetrate into and beyond the surface (FACE) level of Substance and be recognized. Because Substance is DEEP there can be multi-levels of "recognition" as Life ideas pass through the different levels.

THE SPIRIT OF GOD MOVED UPON THE FACE OF THE WATERS

Now the writer of Genesis begins to use a new term as the Intelligence begins its penetration. God is no longer the actor. Instead, the SPIRIT OF GOD takes the stage. What has happened to GOD? GOD is still acting but this new term of reference is a signal that the GOD SEED has now entered another phase of expressive Being (verb).

We get a clue as to the nature of the expression from the Sanskrit definition of SPIRIT. It is defined as "wind." This suggests that the movement of GOD is like wind, or an energy current, so it seems logical that THE SPIRIT OF GOD is the Breath of GOD. The breathing of GOD MOVED the ideas of Life and Substance in MIND in a repetitive rhythmic motion, just like our own breathing!

[See Figure 5]

Figure #5

THE SPIRIT OF GOD MOVED

The TRIANGLE Principle remains intact while it is MOVED in two ways. HEAVEN (idea of Life) moves as currents of vertical energy and EARTH (idea of Substance) moves as currents of horizontal energy. We can observe our own breath and see this same duality of movement. Our breath moves inward and outward in rotating cycles. Both the inward and outward flow of GOD breath constitute the same force, always remaining connected to the original whole, but at the same time acting as polar forces. The Life idea is radiation and the Substance idea is magnetism.

Theology uses the terms "Word" and "Logos" for these moving energies. They are the moving of God Breath that cause creation.

The ideas of Life and Substance can be imagined as spinning, rotating forces. They are moving in MIND. These are the same two moving forces that scientists have discovered in the atom.

Further exploring this passage of scripture, we see the inflow and outflow of GOD SEED breath affecting the FACE of the WATERS. Again, the word FACE implies the "capacity to recognize," so the writer is referring to Substance. The word WATERS indicates another level for the Substance has been reached. Aha! On this newest level the nature of Substance is different than it was in the BEGINNING. It is no longer only a fixed empty vacuum (VOID). Substance is now like WATER; in that it is free flowing energy which is easily convertible.

The scientific name for this Substance is "ether" which can be described as a gaseous liquid. Science defines ether as an all pervading fluid which serves to transmit heat and light waves. Now Substance can receive the heat radiated from the GOD SEED idea. It will be able to receive it as light waves which are being produced from the activity of this moving energy (wind).

Wind moving across water causes ripples or waves. Here too, it is revealing to note that the molecules of water are very cohesive and also polar (positive hydrogen and negative oxygen). The differing frequencies of these ingredients cause a tension between the two which produces a "skin" on the surface of the water. This suggests that creating a form for the idea received will be the result of these polar energies interacting and producing waves of energy upon the Substance.

This fluid state is the result of the GOD breath (Intelligence) moving through the Substance. Since the WATERS (Substance) have FACE (capacity to recognize), this recognition of Intelligent ideas brings change to Substance.

The FACE ("sur-face") OF THE WATERS reflect the light (Intelligence) received. In other words, Substance reflects the idea of Life presented to it. **We have just discovered how MIND works!** As the SPIRIT (wind) OF GOD MOVED, reflection took place. **This is a "mirror image" capacity and is essential to all creation!**

It is comparable to looking into a pool of water and seeing our image reflected back to us. The ether which is a gaseous liquid (Substance) is able to receive the Intelligent Life idea and reflect it back to its source.

We see that GOD'S breathing sets up a continuum of flowing energy currents which will act as a catalyst for creating forms out of Substance. The breath of GOD is as vast as the universe. GOD breathes as galaxies, planets, suns, moons, and stars. GOD breathes as human beings and as a single blade of grass. GOD breathes as an insect and as the atoms in a beach pebble.

Genesis shows that GOD breaths ideas into Substance and they are reflected back clothed in Substance. This is the way the CREATION process operates. Since GOD is the source of these ideas, as well as the moving force within them, it is apparent that GOD energy is acting as the one and only Power, but that Power is split into two aspects. With this polarity, GOD can act as a triune principle, utilizing the all-powerful energy of these two ideas in two opposite ways. An essential observation here is to see that ideas are powerful. Ideas are the core of all experience from the highest level of creation to the lowest. The most important Truth to remember is that **consciousness is the only reality!**

The Bible reveals that MIND is the laboratory of creation but the MIND of Chapter I of Genesis is not the same as our individual MIND. It is the whole, Absolute MIND, or shall we say, the all-knowing consciousness that can act with duality. We shall see how this duality will allow it to eventually become individual MIND. This will happen because it has become two, and can make a mirror image of Itself through self-reflection. Without the initial split of energy to CREATE the TRIANGLE Principle there could be no creation. There would be only the One MIND and individual MIND could not exist. This duality will have many ramifications but the first point to grasp is that once Self-reflection begins, manifestation of the GOD SEED energy can begin.

This act of Self-reflection is illustrated by the following statement in the Bible:

LET THERE BE LIGHT . . . .

[See Figure 6]
[See Figure 7]

Figure #6

LET THERE BE LIGHT

LIGHT is symbolic of the GOD SEED'S intelligent awareness of Self. What is there to be aware of at this point in creation? Only that which already "is." Through Self-reflection the GOD SEED is aware of what "is". Well then, what "is"? A TRIANGLE! LET THERE BE LIGHT means that this Principle of polarity reflects upon Itself, and in so doing, becomes aware of what is in MIND . . . . Itself! This awareness produces an inverted reflection of the TRIANGLE, which has been CREATED. The GOD SEED Trinity now "sees" Itself as a mirrored image of consciousness.

Light is a "wave motion" of radiant energy. It can be defined as perception, awareness, illumination and animation. Because the TRIANGLE can now reflect the original Life and Substance, this is all that GOD needs to bring forth creation. Later, the words of Genesis tell us that GOD MADE everything else out of this MIND Principle. What is MADE will undergo change, but this Principle that was CREATED will remain eternally conscious of the Absolute because that which is CREATED by GOD is eternal and everlasting. Through the operation of this infallible Self-reflecting process everything will be MADE from the two ideas that are in MIND. The TRIANGLE can reproduce them as inverted mirrored images.

The polar energy of the triune Principle can be defined as darkness and light. Everything is within the whole and the whole is within everything. The light is in the darkness and the darkness is in the light. They exist together as one and yet can be discerned in MIND as separate.

Figure #7

UNDERSTANDING THE TRINITY

To summarize up to this point follow the review below:

The word BEGINNING symbolizes MIND.

What is in MIND?

GOD, HEAVEN, EARTH

In other words, these three form a trinity of GOD energy that can be understood in multiple ways. A few basic ways to see these three forces of energy are illustrated. We can think of this trinity as the Power Source of everything acting with both positive active and negative passive currents of energy.

These same three energies are found in the atom. Its neutron at the apex of the TRIANGLE is neutral. The proton is the positive radiating force of the atom and the electron is the negative magnetic force, which attracts the proton. From this union the basic building blocks of matter are produced.

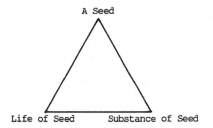

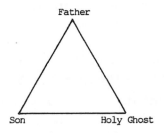

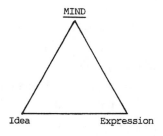

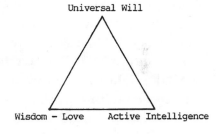

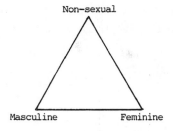

As I read these first few verses of Genesis I began the cry. I was so moved, so in awe of the magnificent power of Creation and its relationship to me! God was not far away and unknowable. The Power to use MIND was already mine. It was with me here and now. There was nowhere I could be without being a part of this Creation process. Genesis had explained to me that God (power Source) uses MIND as the workshop for creation. I lived in MIND and God lived there too. God had seemed to be separate from me, but now I realized that we were together all the time. I did not have to get to God; I was already one with this Infinite Power.

I had not known the power of MIND! Now it was clear to me why Jesus had said, "*Be ye perfect as your Father in Heaven is already perfect.*" God's idea of Life is perfect and it is in MIND, right where I live, move, and have my being! Jesus must have been telling us that we could realize that God perfection because it was available to us in MIND. Now other questions burned in my heart. Perhaps you have similar questions. Why had we not known that we were perfect? Why did we not act with this perfection? Why was this perfect idea of life so foreign to us? We must read on to find these answers.

Chapter 3

WHAT MIND IMAGES IS
PRODUCED AS FORM

We must keep uppermost in our thought process that we are studying the creation story just as we would study mathematics of physics. Don't panic it is much easier than that! I mean that we must understand each principle as we build the whole picture of creation. We are seeking a higher awareness of the process. This part of Genesis will require your concentration. It is not likely that you will remember everything at the first reading but much of it is reiterated throughout our study and gradually you will remember and understand the Creation process and the way your mind works. First let's review what our basic study has so far revealed as essential points for you to understand:

- GOD creates a threefold current of energy in MIND.
- GOD acts only through the law of this principle.
- This GOD principle is the universal law that stands behind all creation.
- Remember that MIND always holds the two ideas, one of Life and the other of Substance, which GOD CREATED. These two ideas are being reflected upon in MIND.
- **Ideas held in MIND will be imaged, manifested and experienced. This is the Law of the TRIANGLE.**

Yes, this is the law! The reflection of the original Life idea produces an image which penetrates into and is received by Substance. As Substance "recognizes" the image it will produce its form. This is how manifestation occurs. The creation story has shown us how this law acts at the Absolute level of MIND. We shall see how other levels of MIND develop and the same process occurs on each level. This is the way all forms, conditions, and experiences come into manifestation. Now we see the nature of MIND! Knowing about this principle of MIND helps us understand why certain things happen to us and why some things are inevitable. They are simply the reflection of thoughts held in MIND. When we observe the operation of this law day by day we learn that we can change conditions only by changing our thought about life and ourselves. When we create new images in MIND we create new circumstances.

This TRIANGLE Principle of Creation is an immutable law!

GOD has CREATED it as a Law of Being (verb). Again, let us remember that according to Genesis this Principle is the only thing CREATED and the only thing GOD needs in order to experience as formed Substance. This is because everything else can be MADE through it. It contains Life and Substance and is Self-reflective. It can produce images and clothe them with forms. The key here is to discern the difference between what is CREATED and what is MADE. Only the TRIANGLE Principle which is CREATED is permanent.

Everything that is MADE out of this TRIANGLE is going to be temporary and constantly changing because consciousness is always changing. Also, there will be different levels of consciousness in MIND. None of these will be alike. However, at the Absolute level of MIND the Principle produces Life and Substance in their pure and absolute state of perfection. This perfection stands behind all the imperfection that will manifest on the different levels of MIND.

In Summary:

- GOD'S law of consciousness manifests what is held in MIND.

- This creative law is infallible, dependable, and unchangeable.
- It is the permanent inexhaustible Source of all creation.
- It is a TRIANGULAR Principle that works just like a Math Principle.

AND GOD SAW THE LIGHT THAT IT WAS GOOD AND GOD DIVIDED THE LIGHT FROM THE DARKNESS.

Continual Self-reflection ensues. The word SAW indicates this is a mental imaging process. GOD SEED perception of Life is called LIGHT because it is active intelligence. GOD SEED perception of Substance is called DARKNESS because it is a waiting, passive vacuum of potential form. Both are multi-dimensional in nature. One is not good and the other evil. They are equal complementary forces and both essential to manifestation. The word GOOD implies that these forces are balanced and therefore fulfilling, satisfying, and glorifying to the creative whole.

What does GOD see? GOOD! What do we see when we self-reflect? Is our concept of Life and Substance fulfilling or lacking? Is it satisfying or disappointing? Is it glorifying or deprecating? Do we believe GOD sends misfortune and disappointment? Don't forget, we live in our consciousness! If life is not what we want we can't blame GOD. Could it be that there is an imbalance between the two forces of energy in our consciousness? Understanding GOD'S Law, it is clear that we must learn to "see" differently and we must begin with the way we see ourselves. As our story continues, we shall see why and how mankind has had difficulty in "seeing" the truth about its existence and has become "unbalanced" in consciousness. When we realize there are many dimensions of consciousness and spheres within spheres, it easy to see how there can be great diversification of awareness.

Remember, the two opposites, LIGHT and DARKNESS did not exist in the BEGINNING. That starting point is the Absolute which is always the perfectly balanced state of MIND even while GOD energy is expressed and experienced on other levels. This Absolute is within all that is CREATED, including us!

At this point in our story, we have reached the place where the mirrored reflection now exists on an extended dimension and this allows a "sense" of separation to be set up in MIND. This illusion of separateness will permit the GOD SEED energy to diversify and take separate forms on many levels of MIND, but the separation is an illusion, just as in any mirrored reflection. However, this illusion will be 'recognized" in MIND on these outer levels as reality.

Realizing that mirrored images seem real explains how it is possible to believe what we see is real when it is not. However, we must also realize that it is possible to experience wholeness even while living a life of illusion and seemingly being separated from GOD or GOOD. Here is the dichotomy of experience and here is the reason we should be glad that immutable law governs our lives. Through it we can find our wholeness by rising in consciousness (a different vantage point) or shall we say "seeing" something or someone differently. When an individual's awareness reaches the level of MIND where it can "recognize" the Absolute whole, the balanced state of perfection will be experienced. It is the law! However, this state of consciousness comes through the practice of choosing to see differently and that practice is a day by day experience.

[See Figure 8]
[See Figure 9]

Figure #8

GOD DIVIDED THE LIGHT FROM THE DARKNESS

As the GOD Breath continuously moves the energies of Life and Substance from the center balanced point of consciousness, the movement causes them to spin and these spinning forces gradually expand their circle of force into a sphere. They interact with each other as two complementary spheres of activity, one within the other. This should make it clear that nothing is flat or one dimensional, but is spherical and multi-dimensional. From our physical viewpoint we are not cognizant of these fields of energy around all things and also our bodies.

These polar energies interact to produce interference patterns. The result of this is that wave patterns of the original ideas of Life are stored so that they can be reflected as images. This is analogous to a hologram that can be described as a photographic plate upon which information is recorded in the form of a wave-front interference pattern. When the pattern is illuminated with the same light under which the information was originally recorded, the wave front is reconstructed in mid-air and is identical to the original. However, the image is a reflection of the original even though it appears to be the original itself.

As we proceed, holograms will be discussed. The main idea at present is that God has created a storage-device TRIANGLE with interference patterns, which will be used to produce any idea imaged in MIND and then provide a form for it from the Substance stored in the TRIANGLE.

Figure #9

SYNTHESIS

The ancient sacred symbol of the East, commonly known as Yin/Yang, is a good illustration of the universal law and it drives home the point of how two can simultaneously be together and apart. The Yin/Yang encompasses the two opposites within a circle of wholeness.

The LIGHT is in the DARKNESS and the DARKNESS is in the LIGHT. The symbol suggests a continuous flowing movement of both aspects. What we see when we look at this symbol depends upon our point of view. How much we see corresponds to our vantage point. So it is with life, since the law has been established that "recognition" is the key to what will be experienced. If the vantage point is LIGHT one cannot see DARKNESS. If the vantage point is DARKNESS one cannot be aware of LIGHT. The opposite does not seem to exist and yet is does exist.

Wow! I hope you feel the same excitement that I felt when this was revealed to me. It was something I never heard of before. It was a gift that I instantly accepted just as I had accepted the secret when I was a child that it was not God's way that people should die. I now realized

THIS TRIANGLE IS ALL THAT GOD CREATED!

It is the only thing God needed for Creation because everything can be made from this TRIANGLE. It is a TRIANGLE because it has three aspects. It contains the Power Source we call God, and perfect Life along with pure unlimited Substance. Everything can be formed and experienced through this TRIANGLE. This TRIANGLE exists in MIND, which is always present, everywhere, and all powerful. Now I understood that this Trinity contained the Secret of life and death. There is nothing more powerful that this TRIANGLE. It will manifest whatever idea of Life has entered into its Substance. It is the foundation and source of all that exists! How does it work?

It works through the action of Self-reflecting individualized consciousness. Science has now recognized this Mind action as the cause of our existence.

At this point it may be beneficial to think about how scientific theories are affirming this part of the Creation Story. Traditional scientific theory assumes that only matter (atoms) is real and all else is secondary phenomena. In other words, objects are real and outside of us. This poses a mechanical universe without spiritual meaning. Today's Quantum Physics gives us an alternative. It presents a universe that does not separate spirit from matter (atoms). It says that there is one ultimate substance from which all matter originates and matter is secondary to consciousness, which is the ground of all being.

Years ago I read the book, "THE SELF AWARE UNIVERSE— How Consciousness Creates the Material World." The author and physicist, Amit Goswami, PhD explains the science-based theory. He reminds us that Albert Einstein theorized that light exists as a quantum and is not just a wave but also a discrete bundle of energy (named photon). Danish physicist Niels Bohr suggested that the world of the atom is full of quantum jumps. It had been taught that an atom resembles a tiny solar system with electrons rotating in orbits around a nucleus. Bohr pointed out that atoms only emit light when electrons jump their orbits.

To quote Amit Goswami, "Although you might be tempted to picture the electrons [of the atom] as a jump from one rung of a ladder to another, the electron makes the jump without ever passing through the space between the rungs. Instead, it seems to disappear at one rung and to reappear at another quite discontinuously. There is more; we cannot tell when a particular electron is going to jump or where it is going to jump."

Scientists have known that light behaves like a wave but the quantum theory insists that light also behaves like a bunch of particles (photons) so light is both wave and particle at the same time. This reminds us that the same dual forces of Genesis are at work here, or could we say it is the same as Yin/Yang?

Now here is another important point: Physicist Werner Heisenberg said the path of the electron comes into existence only when we OBSERVE it! Observation instantly collapses the size of the energy bundle, called a "waveacle" by Einstein, and the collapse is discontinuous. Observing it is called measuring it. Again quoting Goswami:

"Whenever we measure it, the quantum object appears at some single place as a particle. When we are not measuring it the quantum object exists in more than one place at the same time."

In other words, observation affects the particle! They can never be seen as a wave and the particle at the same time! Yet they know it exists when they cannot see it, because it reappears.

The physicists have found that they can either know its momentum or its location but they cannot accurately know both at the same time. Looking at the illustration of the Yin/Yang helps us to see this mystery. If our location is either in the light or in the dark, we can be aware of only what exists where we are, but not what exists in what is not seen. From our space-time vantage point we cannot see the whole since part of whole exists outside of space-time just as MIND exists outside of space and time. It is invisible to us! Quantum objects exist below the atomic level but they reveal the mystery of life that unfolds through science and in Genesis!

The creation story has shown us that invisible substance is the "stuff" that is potential form, which is waiting to "recognize," or "observe" the Life idea and become visible form. We might ask ourselves 'How are we observing, or "taking the measure," of what we see as our life and its potential form? It seems that we must learn to be conscious observers in this mystery of life. Not being able to see both aspects of energy, LIGHT and DARKNESS, or wave and particle, at the same time does not mean that one or the other does not exist. Just as when scientists are looking at the particle they know the wave exists somewhere even though they cannot see it, so too must we know that what we cannot see as "existing" in our life can still be "potential" waiting to be formed.

The Physicists asked, "Is the wave in some transcendental space, outside of space-time?" Their answer is that a "potentia" exists between observations of the electron and this "potentia" cannot be within the material domain of space-time'. Since its momentum and location are not predictable, it does not adhere to the Einstein rule of predictability and speed limit. **Their conclusion was that between observations the electron existed as a possibility wave-form. It had become an archetypical image to be used as a pattern to manifest it.**

Genesis shows us how a vacuum of Substance passively waits to receive the Life ideas and forms them into an image, or archetype. All of this is happening in MIND which is outside of space and time. Science and Theology are gradually becoming one! The creation story has described a process in which the currents of GOD Intelligence (energy) have been stepped down, or shall we say "jumped," or changed orbit, from one frequency of vibration to another, thereby establishing different dimensions of consciousness. Just as any seed, step by step, gives its life and substance to its creation, so does the GOD Source. The stepping down is really an act of mental reflection upon, or observation of, the two ideas of Life and Substance CREATED by GOD.

What does Quantum Physics tell us? After reading Fred Alan Wolf's book, "Taking the Quantum Leap" I was able to make a simplified summary:

1. What one observes appears to depend upon what one chooses to observe.
2. Particles become waves and waves become particles interchangeably. Only one of them can be seen at a time.
3. The universe involves our minds, which hold thoughts about life.
4. The vibrating motion of substance is the root of Quantum mechanics. The observer disrupts the motion and therefore plays an important part in the process of manifesting substance.
5. Our ability to form an image is essential to shaping substance. Our MIND is a mirror image principle.
6. The higher the frequency of vibration, the more powerful the energy emitted, which means more light.
7. Electrons rotate around the nucleus of the atom and store their light (energy) until they leap into another orbit. The higher the jump, the more light they emit.
8. Each observation presents a CHOICE between either an electron or a wave and this cannot be predicted. Thus, our universe is changed by our observation and choice.

Once I understood this, I saw how physicists were discovering the Self-reflective (mirrored image) power of MIND. Using MIND, we cause the substance that receives our idea (image) to vibrate at a certain frequency. This dictates how the idea will be shaped and how much light it will emit. Quantum physics is affirming Genesis law.

Now it seemed possible to me, that since our bodies contain trillions of atoms, all vibrating and emitting light energy, that we can jump into another orbit of MIND. Genesis shows that there are at least seven orbits. They are called "days" in scripture; they are really rays of light.

I never liked math or science until I understood Genesis.

When television introduced me to scientific theories, it was obvious to me that physical laws being probed by physicists were the same laws that were clothed in the symbolic language of Genesis. I used my Genesis yardstick to understand how physical laws could be true. Studying these became extremely interesting. Understanding Quantum Physics left no doubt that "As above, so below." Later on, when researching Ancient Philosophies and Religions, I saw that same maxim in all of them. We might put it this way, "What is invisible to the physical eye is reflected as visible in the manifest realm."

The joy of it is that the God Principle operates in Infinite MIND and humans have consciousness in that same MIND! Quantum theory says that our reality depends upon our choices, which depend upon our thoughts, and our thoughts depend upon what we expect to see or be. Science and Genesis tell us not to depend upon what our five senses report as true. How good it is to know that there are both visible and invisible sides to MIND. There is always that which is hidden behind what appears. The key is to imagine, or form an image of what we want and realize it as true, even if it is not what circumstances would seem to allow. This is why we must learn not to judge by appearances.

Both Genesis and Fred Alan Wolf, in his interesting book about Quantum Physics pose the question:

If the universe is MIND looking at itself, then what is the Self? Wolf's conclusion is that there is really only one SELF, expressing as many. "Out of the One many, and out of the many, One" Certainly this is true according to the Creation story. Now the question comes:

If God is All in All, how exactly does that include us as human beings? Genesis shows us how God's TRIANGLE Principle, reflecting upon Itself, produced the perfect reflection of the Divine Self and this leads us on to finding the answer.

SOUND POWER

The movement of the two ideas of Life and Substance is the inhalation and exhalation of the GOD breath. The Genesis writer makes this clear by using the words CALLED and SAID. This GOD breath is traditionally named the Logos. This Logos can be defined as the Word of GOD. The terms Logos and Word are used interchangeably in Christian theology. Genesis is showing us that an interchange of incoming and outgoing breath, (Logos) acts as a dynamo, or a conductor, in a magnetic field of energy (Substance).

Speech also acts as a conductor of energy on the material, atomic level. Words are the expression of thoughts (LIGHT or intelligence), which manifest in some form as they are received by atomic substance (DARKNESS or matter). Thus, the same Logoic method of creation, which is a conscious reflection upon ideas, along with the issue and moving vibration of breath, acts in our world to produce material forms.

Actually, everyone first creates by the movement of thoughts in MIND. As an idea is reflected upon (observed), an archetype is formed outside of space-time, for the formation of the observation. Then, by using the breath, we speak words about the idea, which moves atoms to produce the archetype held in MIND. The way that individuals create through the vibrating power frequencies of the word is still a mystery to most of humanity. We are told that this process of moving currents of energy has been taught in esoteric Mystery Schools through the Ages. Today, this creative law is studied in metaphysical schools and the power of affirmations and decrees are widely known and practiced.

Proceeding through the Genesis story, we find that the power of the word is used five times. This is indicated by the Words, (AND GOD SAID). Each of these proclamations is the signal that another reflected triangle is appearing. If we line up all five of these triangles side by side, we must alternate the position of their apex point each time, because of their self-reflective nature. If we draw a line from apex point to apex point we are presented with a wave pattern. What is being created here in Genesis is a **sound wave**, which is a vibratory current of energy!

This story is telling us that creation stems from sound caused by moving energy (breath) vibrating at different frequencies. Here, illustrated in a story, is the power of sound wave vibrational frequencies. This story explains how every sound springs from the movement of energy (AND GOD SAID). It shows us that after the first TRIANGLE reflected upon itself, (figure 6), and continued this reflection again and again, the result is the production of sound waves. Thus, two vibrating waves the Absolute Self and Its Self-reflection act as the instrument for GOD MIND to produce something out of Itself.

Since the Bible proclaims that we are made in the IMAGE AND LIKENESS OF GOD, it should not surprise us that we also produce things out of ourselves. This is an important point. Actually, because we move atoms when we speak, we are actively engaged in constantly changing circumstances around us. Do we need to learn how to use the power of sound and speech in more productive and harmonious ways? Indeed, we do!

Here again, let's consider the wave and the particle. Physicists cannot predict where the invisible particle will reappear. This is because their observation of it causes it to disappear or spread out before reappearing. Why is this so? Genesis gives us the answer . . . . because we observe with consciousness and according to the state of consciousness at any given moment the place of reappearance is established. Since consciousness is changing moment by moment, there is always a new beginning for every particle which cannot be predicted.

We should always be aware of this as we observe and then follow through with the speaking of words to express our conscious thoughts, and that we are moving matter (atoms). This is why our words have so much power. The old adage: "sticks and stones may break my bones but words can never harm me" is not true. The spoken word builds thought forms that can imprison us or those around us. We sow our words, which are vibratory patterns, in the soil of invisible Substance and as they are received, they produce forms. Both the Bible and Quantum Physics insist that our words return to us. We cannot know exactly where they will reappear in our lives, but they will, just as the particle unpredictably reappears. Words that are harmful and fearful build limiting circumstances just as words of love and compassion can build positive ones.

AND GOD CALLED THE LIGHT DAY, AND THE DARKNESS HE CALLED NIGHT. AND THE EVENING AND THE MORNING WERE THE FIRST DAY

As the breathing Word is used (CALLED), cycles begin within this

Solar Logos. Hence, the term FIRST DAY is used. They are named DAYS in the story. These DAYS will each lend a unique quality (ray of LIGHT or intelligence) to the expression of Life and Substance. They give variety and interest to creation. Each quality will predominate at certain times and recede at others as the DAYS (rays of energy) rotate in cycles. This cyclic movement will govern everything that is made so that continual renewal can eventually bring a perfected condition and expression.

AND GOD SAID, LET THERE BE FIRMAMENT, AND DIVIDED THE WATERS WHICH WERE UNDER THE FIRMAMENT FROM THE WATERS WHICH WERE ABOVE THE FIRMAMENT, AND IT WAS SO.

As we continue with the story of creation, we see that the moving breath, having been permanently established on the Solar level, causes an actual separation, resulting in the establishment of a lower Planetary level. This happens because there is an illusion of separation in consciousness. This passage also shows that the Logos or breath is used (SAID) to establish a point of stability and balance (FIRMAMENT) between these Solar and Planetary levels.

At this point in the story the Substance that forms these two levels is called WATERS because its condition is no longer fixed. On the Planetary level, Substance now has an unlimited potential to form according to the idea presented to it. The word WATERS emphasizes that Substance is poured out of MIND as easily as liquid. The unlimited energies of Life and Substance are being poured out from the Solar Logos to the Planetary Logos which are each the breathing apparatus of the GOD SEED on their particular level. The Planetary Logos releases through sound, the breath (SAID) whatever intelligent idea is imaged. Thus, through continual reflective observation and the power of moving currents of energy, Life can be expressed through Substantive forms. This might be a good place to pause and think about what kind of image of YOURSELF are you holding in MIND?

[See Figure 10]

Figure #10

LET THERE BE FIRMAMENT AND DIVIDED THE WATERS

The ideas of Life and Substance pour out from the creative Principle as they are reflected upon. Creation is all a process of Self-reflection through mirrored inverted images. Actually, the FIRMAMENT acts in the same way as a camera lens, since it inverts any image and thereby changes the perspective, but it also stabilizes ideas. Although the ideas are now free, there must remain in MIND the ability to concentrate upon any idea in order to bring it into manifestation. Therefore, a point of stability has been established between the inner level (Solar and Spiritual) and the outer layers of consciousness (Planetary and material). On the Planetary level matter will be the agent of expression for ideas and the place of balance between matter and ideas of Spirit is called FIRMAMENT.

This explains why in order to create an idea, we must concentrate. If our concentration is broken, we must again focus upon it in order to stabilize it in MIND, or we will fail to manifest our ideal. The greater our power of concentration, the faster our idea will manifest. Without this placement of the FIRMAMENT between the inner and outer levels of consciousness, MIND energy would be scattered and there could be no organization of energy for material forms.

This portion of Scripture shows us that no matter how diversified the ideas of Life and Substance may become, there is a permanent point of equilibrium established in MIND that acts as the foundation for their expression. This perfect balance is necessary since reflection upon the ideas will be subject to change as they begin to move through successive lower levels of MIND. Without it, perfection would never be possible in the manifest world. More about this as we proceed.

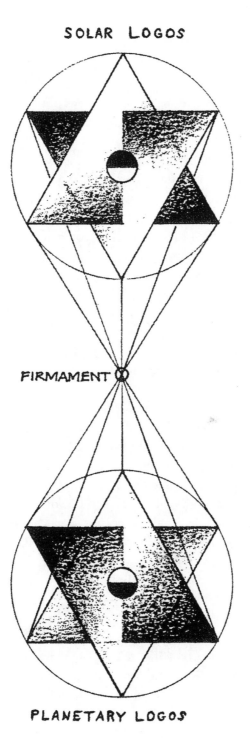

SOLAR LOGOS

FIRMAMENT

PLANETARY LOGOS

Another aspect of universal law is revealed in the previous passage about the division of WATERS. From the extended levels of MIND, the perception of the original ideas will not be as clear as it is on the FIRST level (DAY). It is the perfect one. Each successive level of creation will reproduce more Self-reflections but because the levels of consciousness will always be changing, they will not be perfect. The process of successive mirrored images now begins and we will see the DAYS unfold. The Genesis writer used the words UNDER AND ABOVE in this passage. The mirrored image can be only partially perceived from the UNDER side of FIRMAMENT, while the original appears as whole and perfect from the ABOVE side. According to Genesis this is how the universal law will operate.

Here again, we can apply what we have learned from Quantum Physics. It seems the whole creation story is physics, showing us both the physical side and the spiritual side of creation! Or shall we say, showing us what is both in space-time and what is outside of it. The two different observations of what exists may also be equated to placing an object above a mirror that is laid on a table. By holding the object just above the mirror and looking in the mirror, we can only see the reflected underside. The whole object cannot be seen in the mirror. However, a view of the object from above reveals not only the partially reflected image, but also the whole object. The view from the top (ABOVE) is a very different one than the view from the bottom (UNDER).

This illustrates why looking at only the reflection from below limits our perception of what really exists. Part of what exists is, to us, in an invisible realm. Applying this to our own life, we can realize that from our human, material perspective we have only a partial view of everything. We observe only from the UNDER side of the point of balance (FIRMAMENT). At the same time, however, from the ABOVE level, the spiritual, the whole of things can be seen.

AND GOD CALLED THE FIRMAMENT HEAVEN

The point of balance (FIRMAMENT) between these flowing spheres of energy is given another name. Remembering that GOD CREATED an idea of Life symbolized in the first line of the Bible as HEAVEN, the fact that the FIRMAMENT is only CALLED

HEAVEN but is not HEAVEN itself should not be missed here. The FIRMAMENT is not the original Life idea but it does reflect that perfect idea which exists in the original Principle of Creation. Therefore, it is a perfect place of stability for the Planetary level of manifestation.

To summarize what has happened, a mirror image is produced as the two ideas pass through the FIRMAMENT CALLED HEAVEN. Here, the UNDER side is the opposite of the ABOVE side. This means that the GOD SEED original energies will now first observe Life from the UNDER side and secondly, from the spiritual, unseen side. This is an important point. Since the UNDER side is only partially whole there is a presumption of need that is now experienced. From this UNDER vantage point MIND acts as a vacuum waiting to be filled. Actually, the **FIRMAMENT acts as a lens through which the rays of light (ideas) can pass.**

One might ask why this perception of need is necessary. The answer is that if there was no such perception there would be no urge to manifest forms to fill the need. Genesis shows us that the experience of Life and Substance on the lower Planetary levels of MIND will be from this inverted point of view. This explains why we judge from appearances rather than from the ideas that cause them. Once we know that appearances are deceiving we can understand that relying upon them and believing that they bring us either joy or sorrow, keeps us ignorant of their cause. Hence, we must learn how to let go of our attachment to outer things and dependence upon others. We can grow to understand that we ourselves are a creative principle that can change conditions by changing our beliefs about ourselves.

LET THE WATERS UNDER THE HEAVEN BE GATHERED TOGETHER UNTO ONE PLACE AND LET THE DRY LAND APPEAR.

On the UNDER side of the FIRMAMENT the Life idea, which is intelligence, or LIGHT, moves in a gyrating motion making a wave of energy. This establishes a regular, repetitive, vibrating frequency. Quantum science (below the atomic level) which Genesis is now explaining, tells us that light behaves both like a wave and a particle at the same time. They are not two, but one. A good way to understand this is to take a sock and turn it inside out. It appears different on the inside but it is not a separate sock, it is the same sock turned inside out and you cannot see both the inside and outside at the same time. It is not two socks but one! More about this oneness will be understood clearly as we proceed.

In order to see how the dual forces of the GOD SEED interact, we must remember that the nature of Substance (DRY LAND) is to receive the Life idea. In other words, the wave moves or "plays" across that passive, stationary bundle of energy (particle). Quantum physics insists that stationary patterns confined within atoms regenerate themselves, repeating the same performance over and over again. This should be no surprise to us, who have seen this same action taking place in Genesis. It has shown us that the creative process is one of continual renewal and expansion of electromagnetic energy, which takes place by reflecting upon itself over and over again.

It is well to remember that the characteristics of atoms are defined as constant stability, the ability to identify with one another (discriminate), and the ability to regenerate and renew. These are the same characteristics of the Original triune Principle of the GOD SEED.

At this point in the creation story and at this level of creation we see patterns for material structures forming so that existence in a physical realm can begin for the GOD SEED. The appearance of DRY LAND, the current name for Substance, means that its fluid, convertible state has changed again into what can now be described as bundles of light particles. These are the beginning of matter.

[See Figure 11]

Figure #11

LET DRY LAND APPEAR

This drawing reviews the process for making a permanent atom.

The original circle is the whole. We call it the GOD SEED unit of energy, or shall we say, the Divine Absolute Consciousness. It creates a triune Principle to disperse Its dual energy. Through this TRIANGLE a thread, or stream of energy, is released from Its nucleus which continues on to the next level.

At the next level the polar energies of the TRIANGLE reflect upon themselves. This produces a perfect reflection that is a replica of the original. Now, with their movement, their polarity expands as circles or spheres, each moving opposite the other.

The stream of Intelligent energy continues to move to the next phase of development.

Here, the spherical vibrating rotation of negative energy, is the circling movement around the positively charged nucleus. The association between these two forces forms a permanent atom for the Planetary level of expression of Life and Substance.

Science tells us that an atom is a spheroidal form containing within itself a nucleus of life. It has three characteristics: rotary motion, discriminative power, and the ability to develop. This applies not only to material atoms but also to the Planetary permanent atom. This suggests that we each have a permanent atom of our own that serves as the regenerative, renewing source for our eternal existence!

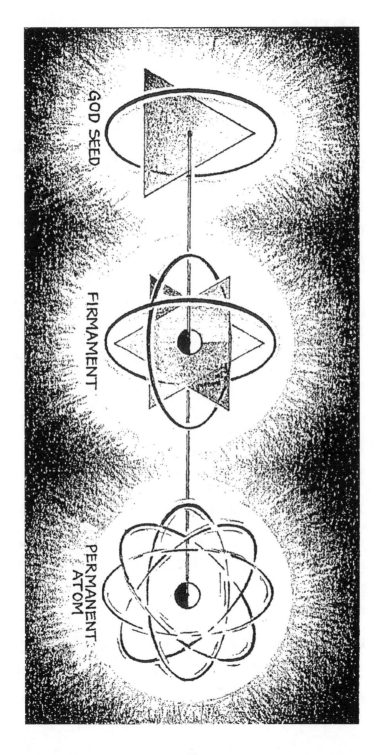

INVOLUTION AND EVOLUTION

The science of Genesis has been describing the descending states of consciousness which is the involution of Spirit into matter. After the descent, evolution begins an ascending movement of states of consciousness. Don't forget, this is all taking place MIND, therefore, consciousness is electromagnetic energy. Humanity is at the present time, slowly ascending from the lower reflected levels to the higher ones. With every new state of awareness, that energy causes an expanded perspective which brings an explosion of mental energy, or the birth of reorganized energy. Here again, we could say in the "Quantum language," with every new observation of life comes an expansion or spreading out of the particle. This activity is unseen but its energy returns to us as higher understanding of life and through visible, tangible circumstances.

Genesis now names four elements that will be involved in the creation of matter. This is indicated by the plural word WATERS. The two have now become four because of the reflective process. These four elements have been observed by both physical and spiritual scientists and they can be described as moving energy:

* The etheric sphere (element of fire)
* The mental sphere (element of air)
* The astral sphere (element of water)
* The material atomic sphere (element of earth).

The Bible symbolism used for these elements is as follows:

* EARTH
* GRASS YIELDING HERBS AFTER ITS OWN KIND
* SEAS
* TREE YIELDING FRUIT

The Bible symbolism used for the nature of consciousness is as follows:

* MOVING CREATURES
* WINGED FOWL

* LIVING CREATURES
* CATTLE
* CREEPING THINGS
* BEASTS

All of these describe the nature of the ideas of Life and Substance as they descend through lower frequencies of vibration. They also represent the vibratory states that will serve for the formation of the mineral, vegetable, and animal kingdoms through which the original Intelligence (LIGHT) will have to penetrate before it can build a suitable physical vehicle through which to experience Life and Substance on the lower level. This vehicle will be a physical body made of the four elements and it will serve as a temple for GOD.

The important thing to know is that these terms are used symbolically to describe the basis for the formation of a multi-dimensional Planetary system with its inhabitants. Each dimension has Beings, all expressing Life and Substance according to their degree of awareness about the two original ideas. Every inhabitant of the system is multi-dimensional, having multiple states of consciousness in the One MIND. However, human beings, whose awareness has been limited only to the outer sphere of activity, have no knowledge of this multiplicity. We shall see how and why this limitation occurs as we proceed. Actually, all physical forms have surrounding "bodies," or fields of vibrating energy, that are not known to the five lower physical senses. In the creation story the same symbolism that describes the four spheres also serves to establish that there will be four lower bodies for every individualization of the GOD SEED which is about to take place. The four are as follows:

EARTH = physical body of atomic substance (earth element)

SEAS = emotional or astral body, ever moving, waving energy (water element)

GRASS YIELDING HERBS AFTER ITS OWN KIND = lower mental body, yielding air images according to thoughts (air element)

TREE YIELDING FRUIT = etheric body, fiery archetype of the

physical body (fire element). This is a web of interlacing channels formed from a composite of all the elements of matter. This is the frame around which the dense physical body is formed. It acts as focal point for radiating emanations which stimulate the physical matter.

[See figure 12]

Figure #12

THE FOUR ELEMENTS OF CREATION

Following the chart, we see the Absolute Source of energy radiates four elements to make up the ABOVE level of MIND, which are the higher spheres They are then reflected to make up the UNDER level. Each expresses the character of one of the four elements.

★In the higher spheres, the dual energy flows out of the Absolute, acting as a reflective Principle and thereby expressing four aspects of the original energy, which are now defined as elements.

★On the highest level the element of fire (radiation of heat).

★On the next level the element of air (thought) is used.

★The duality continues to flow and involve itself in the next level.

★Through Self-reflection comes the water element (feeling), which is magnetism.

★Stepping itself down even further, the earth element stabilizes its diffused energy to form a permanent atom.

This illustrates how the higher spheres are reflected and appear as the lower spheres, using the same four elements to form lower "bodies", or fields of energy. Also note the illusive veil, or curtain of consciousness, between the higher and lower spheres, which veils the higher from the lower, or shall we say the ABOVE from the UNDER. You may have also noticed that this diagram resembles illustrations of the human spinal column with seven charkas. Surely, the physical creation follows the patterns set up on the inner levels.

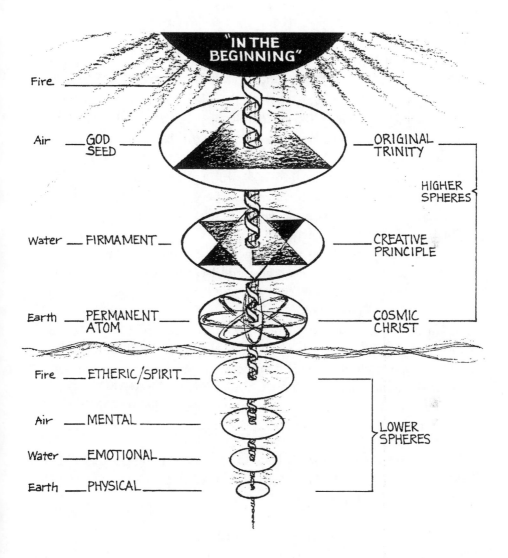

LET US MAKE MAN IN OUR OWN IMAGE AND LIKENESS

Question: Who is us?

The GOD SEED is speaking to, or reflecting upon Its two aspects of flowing energy. GOD can only "know" or "be" on manifest levels through Self-reflection, which is really the interaction of energy between these two aspects. This is the law that has been established by the GOD SEED and there can be no departure from this law. The same is true for us since we are made in the IMAGE AND LIKENESS OF GOD. Actually, we are the stuff of the GOD SEED in a continual state of Self-reflection, or shall we say, the interaction between the higher and lower aspects of our being. By using the method of interaction between two different frequencies of energy the Bible is now going to show us how the One GOD reproduces as many gods, just as one seed reproduces as many seeds. We are each one of those gods! We are gods in training! We will eventually realize this Truth through the process of Self-reflection that is always going on within us.

In this first chapter of Genesis, even though a MAN is MADE, a human being is not yet made. At this level of creation in our story, MAN is a pattern of LIGHT. This MAN is the "Only begotten Son" of the Bible and can be called the Cosmic Christ. This MAN has all the attributes of the original Principle and will operate by the same laws of regeneration and Self-reflection.

LET THEM HAVE DOMINION OVER THE FISH OF THE SEA AND THE FOWL OF THE AIR AND OVER THE CATTLE AND OVER ALL THE EARTH.

This passage shows that there will be more than one MAN on the Planetary level. Note the word THEM. In one passage we are told that MAN will be MADE, but now that MAN is referred to as THEM. Evidently, the MAN made from the permanent atom of the Cosmic Christ is able to multiply just as atoms can multiply. It is the law! We are going to see exactly how this multiplication comes about. This MAN is given DOMINION over all the EARTH (Substance). At this level of MIND, Substance is described symbolically as FISH, FOWL, CATTLE, ETC. This illustrates the different ways energy will express, such as FISH (water-emotions), FOWL (air-mental), CATTLE (earth-forms). In other words, the Planetary MAN is to be MADE in a particular way, a way that will give him authority over Substance in all its expressions. He is to rule over his emotional nature, his lower mental nature, and his physical body. Mind over matter!

[See Figure 13]

Figure #13

MAN IS A LIVING PRINCIPLE

Now it is time for us to use our imagination to picture this MAN that has been MADE IN THE IMAGE AND LIKENESS OF GOD. Going back to the BEGINNING we recall that the GOD SEED produces two roots to establish the triangular principle.

Following the illustration of Figure #13 from the bottom up, see the polar energy being exchanged and Self-reflection occurring, producing a perfect reflection. This is the starting point for the Solar Logos activity that works as GOD breath, through Its perfect Self-reflection, the Cosmic Christ. From this Christ, flows the One Intelligence, or Cosmic Will.

Don't forget that because of the reflective action, an inversion happens and the two original ideas of Life and Substance take the opposite position on the TRIANGLE at this lower level. Now experience will first come from the perspective of the Substance idea and secondly from the perspective of the Life idea. In the BEGINNING the opposite was true. At this cross point, (FIRMAMENT), the exchange of these polar energies gathers Life and Substance (electrons and protons) to produce the permanent atom.

It is the counterpoint of the Absolute level of the GOD SEED which now will be able to act at the Planetary level. We can think of it as the permanent atom which holds the whole pattern, or archetype, for MAN. This permanence is the central essence of the Cosmic Christ or MAN of Genesis I.

Therefore, this Cosmic Christ exists eternally as the archetype in MIND and we all have consciousness in that One MIND. We can picture this MAN as a tree or pattern of living energy.

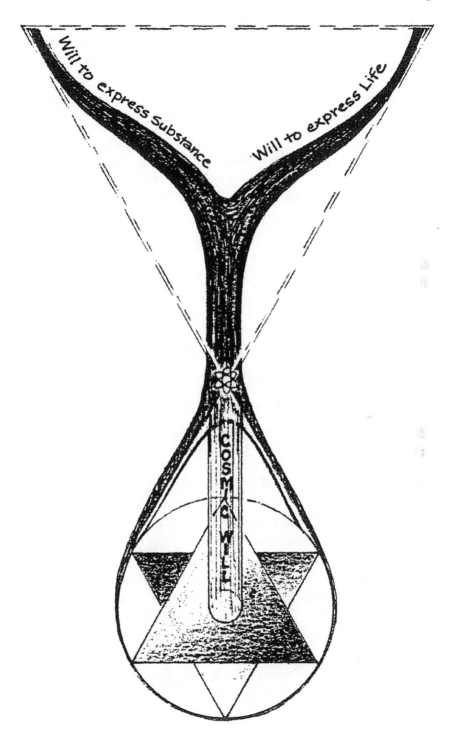

All that has proceeded has been an effort to explain that because of the exchange of two energies manifestation can happen. However, a sense of separation between the two presents a natural urge for union with its polar opposite. We have seen how this urge brought about the penetration of the Life idea (LIGHT) into the (DARKNESS) of the Substance idea. The result of this penetration was the birth of the Cosmic Christ. This is an illustration of the masculine and feminine nature of GOD and all of Its Creation.

The story reiterates what brings about the birth of offspring in the material world. The permanent atom, or seed, is conceived in the womb of universal Substance, gestation occurs, and the Life and Substance contained in the atom are eventually released from the WATERS (Substance). The offspring is a perfect reflection of GOD and we have called this newborn the Cosmic Christ. The Christ will act as the perfect pattern for countless offspring yet to come. It is out of this Cosmic Christ that we have spawned as both spiritual and material beings. It is the "Father" within. As the Master Jesus proclaimed, *"It is not I, but the Father within me that doeth the works."*

The perfect MAN is the pattern for all men (used in the generic sense). In the Old Testament this Being is spoken of as the LORD GOD and also as JEHOVAH. He is not a human being, nor is he GOD in the Absolute sense, but he is the "only begotten Son" of GOD, the offspring.

We do not know what causes GOD to be, nor do we seek to define GOD, but we do know how GOD acts. Genesis shows this clearly.

GOD acts as a reflective creative Principle of MIND (a law) that brings forth a Son.

This Son is like His parent in that He is also a reflective Principle, able to reproduce Himself. Out of the ONE will come many as sons of GOD are born. The experience and expression of the GOD SEED now begins on the lower levels of creation, now that they have been established according to Cosmic law and will operate through the Cosmic Christ.

At the present stage of evolution mankind cannot fathom the whole nature of this Son, but for the purpose of understanding this story, refer again to illustration #13. This Son is a field of living energy, shaped like a tree, having a trunk with two branches. Why? This is because He is made in the IMAGE AND LIKENESS OF GOD, which acts with duality. Therefore, the Son is also triune in nature and is shaped like a TRIANGLE! Since there are three basic aspects to the original GOD SEED Principle, this Christ MAN that has been born also embodies these three aspects. They begin to manifest at this point in the story as follows:

SO GOD CREATED MAN IN HIS OWN IMAGE, IN THE IMAGE OF GOD CREATED HE HIM; MALE AND FEMALE CREATED HE THEM.

If GOD is a living Principle of MIND, so too is the offspring. Like GOD Principle, the MAN will be able to Self-reflect and thereby reproduce on the lower levels all that is held in MIND on the upper levels. The MAN is a duplication of the CREATED Principle and is a perfect copy. Therefore, this Cosmic Christ is not only MADE but He is CREATED, or permanent. We shall see how everything else comes out of this MAN that will produce and parent all manifestation.

This MAN is GOD'S IMAGE and therefore, expresses both the MALE and the FEMALE attributes of the Original. This passage does not mean that GOD MADE males and females, (not at this level of creation), it means that GOD produced this Cosmic MAN to be the pattern with both the male and female qualities inherit in its nature, which are the same two original aspects of energy within the GOD SEED TRIANGLE. Later, we see that this innate duality causes another separation at a still lower level, so that males and females do separately come into manifestation, but each expresses both characteristics with one being dominant over the other.

This part of Genesis tied up a lot of loose ends for me. I was convinced for the first time that I really was made in the image and likeness of God. The word "image" meant just that. Now I saw how I was a mirror Image of God, not as a human being, but as a Divine Principle of MIND. Therefore, I was "like" God because I used the Principle in the same way that God used it. I could create what I concentrated upon through

this Principle of MIND action. That was the part of me that was invisible. But hold on here! The physical part of me could not be ignored. Now I needed to know how I became a physical human body. Genesis explains that too.

This brings us to the end of the first Chapter of Genesis. No attempt has been made in this interpretation to comment upon every facet of this Cosmic story. Hopefully, enough has been said to convince you that the traditional religious GOD concept is a far departure from the one presented here. The second chapter of Genesis describes how a human being began its evolution.

I want to point out that there was a long period, perhaps millions of years, before the formation of the physical body, as we know it today, took place on this plane. So far, the Bible has described the birth of the Archetype, or we could say the pattern, for mankind. This Archetype is the Cosmic Christ. It has also described the elements required to produce material form. All of this is being produced out of a TRIANGLE of energy established in Infinite MIND. It operates through Self-reflection of its permanent Life and Substance. Next, the Bible skips to the period in evolution when the elements for a physical body were ready to be formed.

Chapter 4

HOLOGRAPHIC LIVING SOULS

M any Bible scholars surmise that the first and second chapters of Genesis are two different stories of creation. This cannot be the case if one understands their symbols. Actually, the second chapter is not another story but a continuation of the same story at a later stage of development.

We are introduced to another level of consciousness. Genesis does so by no longer referring either to GOD (the Absolute) or to the SPIRIT OF GOD, (wind or breath) but to the LORD GOD. Since the word LORD means "governor" or "law," this shows that the offspring will always act through the Law of MIND that has been established in the involution process. It will govern on the material level.

THE LORD GOD FORMED MAN OF THE DUST OF THE GROUND AND BREATHED INTO HIS NOSTRILS THE BREATH OF LIFE, AND MAN BECAME A LIVING SOUL. (Gen.2:7)

MAN is FORMED by LORD GOD. MAN is formed from the Self-reflective nature of the Cosmic Christ MAN, which is to say, by the Cosmic Law (LORD). The Law is the TRIANGLE. It radiates its Life as "I" and magnetizes and forms that Life as "AM."

The cyclic breath of the LORD GOD (law of MIND) establishes that consciousness of "I AM" in the Cosmic Christ MAN, called a LIVING SOUL. This means the Life takes on consciousness of itself.

The term, DUST OF THE GROUND indicates that Substance

is now at the sub-atomic level where it can begin the FORMED process to produce individualized LIVING SOULS. This means that the FORMED MAN is to be the reflection of the Cosmic Christ (the first MAN) and will also know an individual identity. These LIVING SOULS will embody the same reproductive nature as the parent.

However, because the separate identity of "I AM" exists, this will cause many limitations in consciousness. We must not let this fact alarm us, since we have seen that the nature of the Divine energy is Self-giving, or sacrificial love. All will be well! Genesis has already shown us a progression of Self-giving:

- The GOD SEED gives Its own Life and Substance to become a Creative Principle.
- The TRIANGLE Principe gives Its own Life and Substance, to MAKE MAN (Cosmic Christ), which then is pronounced as Its perfect and permanent creation by using the word CREATED.
- The Cosmic Christ as a LIVING SOUL is the perfect reflection of its parent.
- Now, as the LIVING SOUL, we shall see how this Cosmic MAN will also sacrifice Life and Substance to become many souls on the atomic level and each offspring will have the "I AM" consciousness.

An ordinary seed is a good analogy for this progressive self-giving. A seed sacrifices its life and substance to become a living organism which will produce many seeds. Each seed produced is an individualization of its parent seed and embodies the same principle of reproduction. Thus, seeds in our material world serve as evidence that this sacrificial giving is the law of the universe. This universal law could be stated as follows:

That which is to be must come from that which already exists

This is the law because everything came from that which already existed as God MIND energy. All Creation must follow the same pattern of action.

Ponder on this. That which we are to be, must come from what we are! Our present existence forms the future and what seems to be an ending is really a new beginning. Therefore, every death is a birth and every birth is a death. This means that what makes up our present consciousness will continually regenerate and become another bundle of energy that can be identified as our consciousness at another time. Let's take a moment to apply this to our everyday lives. Since all of creation takes place in MIND, experience has to be the result of consciousness at any given time. Thoughts about conditions in our lives are the seeds for new "organisms," or new patterns for experiences. The familiar is continually sacrificed for the unfamiliar because our thoughts are always changing.

Of course, consciousness is not material but exists outside of space-time. Here we are reminded again of the interplay between the wave and the particle. When observing one or the other, one will disappear and is outside space-time. Both the wave and the particle cannot be seen at the same time, but both exist, one in the material realm and the other outside of space-time. We can be sure of that because there is always a reappearance of that which was unseen. This is the continual renewing process of creation.

This awareness of how this law works should help us be less resistant to ever changing conditions in our lives. Nonresistance to circumstances helps make all changes easier. Knowing this law, should also make it clear that every individual will undergo self-sacrifice in order to reach successive levels of expression. The entire Bible is about this sacrifice of self which is continually taking place. It is a process of the old giving way for the new.

[See Figure 14]
[See Figure 15]

Illustration #14

AND MAN BECAME A LIVING SOUL

To mark our place in the Genesis story, think again about the mirror image of MAN He is a pattern of LIGHT, or energy, in the form of a tree with two branches. Now, place the LIVING SOUL in that image.

This LIVING SOUL is conscious of being individual. The Cosmic breath at this stage of creation is experiencing "I AM."

Once Self-consciousness is operational in the MAN, individualization becomes possible. Breath by breath, atom by atom, Substance is being gathered so that many souls can be generated from this Cosmic Christ MAN. Since this Cosmic Christ Man is the perfect reflection of Its Parent and therefore has the power of reproduction, or shall we say, make copies of Itself.

This "Only Begotten Son of God" acts as a lens through which is focused Life and Substance. This focusing process reflects the LIGHT of the Original God energy pattern into other dimensions below the Absolute. In this way, God can experience on many levels.

AND MAN BECAME A LIVING SOUL

Figure #15

THE SOUL'S POLARITY PRODUCES TWO TREES

AND THE LORD GOD PLANTED A GARDEN . . . . THE TREE OF LIFE ALSO IN THE MIDST OF THE GARDEN AND THE TREE OF KNOWLEDGE OF GOOD AND EVIL.

How will the LIVING SOUL become many souls? Through its innate creative Principle the soul has polarity and can reproduce this polarity. This is why there are two TREES. Each pole of activity is called a TREE. Without the polarity, multiplication would be impossible, with it, one dimension of experience can become many dimensions.

The Bible gives us names for the TWO TREES. One is called the TREE OF LIFE and the other, the TREE OF KNOWLEDGE OF GOOD AND EVIL. These are two states of consciousness in the SOUL that live in the GARDEN of MIND. One is the conscious awareness of whole, regenerating, eternal Life and the other is only the KNOWLEDGE about this LIFE, which will vacillate between the two opposites of GOOD AND EVIL.

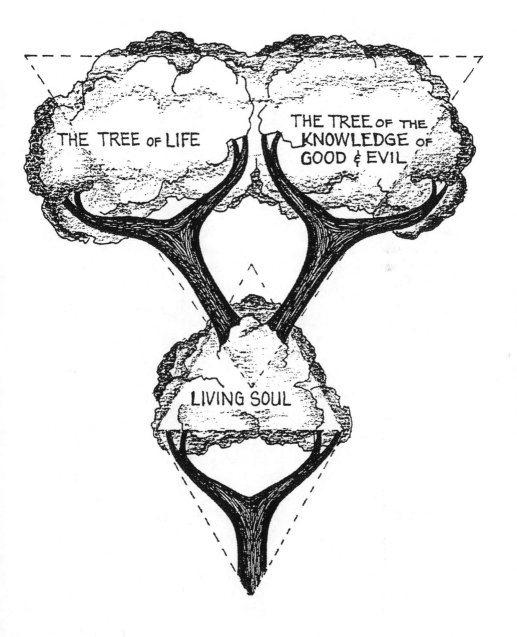

AND THE RIVER WENT OUT OF EDEN TO WATER THE GARDEN AND FROM THENCE IT WAS PARTED AND BECAME INTO FOUR HEADS.

Notice the word FOUR. Two now become FOUR. RIVER implies that the original breath is a continual flowing current which supplies the energy needed in the GARDEN. We can think of it as currents or waves of energy moving the Life idea through Substance, which gives it shape and form. This activity of MIND is indicated by the name EDEN which has also been called GARDEN. EDEN has the double meaning of "time" and "pleasure." In Hebrew this GARDEN of EDEN is called "Gan-heden" with "Gan" meaning, "an organized sphere of activity and "heden" taking on the double meaning of "an eternity" along with "beauty and pleasure." Thus, by putting all these meanings together, the GARDEN OF EDEN is a symbol for an organized sphere of consciousness that functions eternally in a pleasurable and beauteous state.

This level of MIND (GARDEN) is the reflection of the FIRMAMENT CALLED HEAVEN (the permanent atom) on a higher level. The RIVER currents are actually the Will of the GOD SEED which has PARTED INTO FOUR HEADS for the purpose of further expansion. Here, at the atomic level of consciousness, we see regeneration of the four elements already established as fire, air, water, and earth. They are to be the ingredients for the forms which are about to manifest as atomic matter. Their expansion has been from the original One, which became two, and now FOUR. Thus, we see that the LIVING SOUL has the capacity to multiply and we are reminded of the law and decree of GOD in Genesis, "be fruitful and multiply."

Suddenly, the names ADAM and EVE appear in the text along with the TWO TREES. Once again, new names signal the introduction of a new condition for Substance. ADAM and EVE are the original polar aspects of the creative Principle at this lower level of consciousness of the GOD SEED. Logically, ADAM is the original masculine aspect of that SEED, earlier called Life, and EVE is the original feminine aspect called Substance, which is always ready to receive the Life idea.

Logically, we can discern that with each successive lowering of MIND action, mental energy has been lowered in vibration. Mental activity is electrical energy and vibrates at a frequency that is indicative to the level of awareness about any given idea. With each descending level, consciousness has been funneled into ever narrowing perimeters. At the individualization level, awareness is narrowly focused as it is funneled (MOVED) into the correspondingly lower vibration of Substance. At this lower vibrating frequency, the individualized Self-conscious Christ experiences Itself as many individual souls and can no longer fully "know" Itself as it exists in the higher vibration of mental activity. This lower frequency receives only KNOWLEDGE about the higher Self. Therefore, the real Christ Self-identity is not comprehended.

ADAM represents this extension of consciousness and is the masculine aspect of the GOD SEED. He is not a person, but is the thinking and mental activity in the soul. Here, the thinking process is anchored at the concrete, material level of MIND and is esoterically called the lower mental body, or field of energy.

The Christ pattern of Self still exists outside of space-time and is really a higher mental body (field of mental energy) that is directly connected to the lower mental body by a thread or stream of consciousness that is WATERING the GARDEN where the two aspects of GOD SEED energy now abide. The point of all this is that the mental body (ADAM) is really the original GOD Intelligence which has passed through all the descending levels and is now expressing in a limited way, but still retains a stream or current of awareness about the truth of being. This RIVER of Divine Intelligence maintains, governs and sustains Life on what will now become a material manifest level of being.

Genesis II describes how limited this GOD Intelligence has become at the material level when it states that ADAM is put into a DEEP SLEEP. Obviously, the descent of the Life idea into this realm causes mental inertia; the vibration of the ADAM consciousness is sluggish because it is imprisoned within material atoms. ADAM represents the inert state of awareness that will restrict the soul for a long time before it fully awakens to the truth about itself. The Bible shows us that the awakening will come through an evolutionary scheme which will be outlined later in this book.

While in a DEEP SLEEP, a RIB is taken from ADAM. This word DEEP reminds us of how it was used initially in the earlier text of the Bible. You will recall that EARTH (idea of Substance) was described as being VOID and DEEP to illustrate its capacity to receive the idea of Life (HEAVEN). Here the DEEP SLEEP of ADAM indicates that the Life idea has reached the DEEP, lower, recesses of Substance. Even at this level, the polarity of the Principle still prevails as ADAM and EVE illustrate these two poles of energy. EVE and ADAM are not separate entities but two aspects of atomic energy (matter). They cannot be separate since the nature of the Principle is always ONE, becoming two, and acting as three, in order to reproduce Itself. This truth was given to us in the first line of the Bible. The Bible reiterates this point when ADAM describes EVE:

THIS IS BONE OF MY BONE, AND FLESH OF MY FLESH.

Here we need to remind ourselves again that everything in this story is taking place in MIND and the words are symbolic. The symbolism of the word BONE and FLESH must not fool us into thinking that a material human body has yet been produced. Therefore, the appearance of EVE only signifies that the Substance she represents is ripe for the manifestation of a material human body, (along with other types of material forms). EVE is the feeling nature; which can feel and experience the individualized Life idea. Out of the WATERS (name for Substance at the higher level which is now called EVE) a body, or field of energy that can respond to and express the Life idea, comes into being.

A physical body with a sense nature and a dual nervous system will be necessary for the material experience and EVE is the Substance that is ready to become just such a body of FLESH AND BONE. She is an emotional body, or astral field of energy (outside of space-time) that is connected to the mental bodies by the same RIVERS or currents of energy that WATER the GARDEN of mental activity. Every individual Christ soul will use the EVE aspect (FEMALE) as the ability to feel both physically and emotionally on the lower level. She is the "HELPMATE" of ADAM, (MALE, mental nature). Therefore, every thought will be connected to a feeling and every feeling will express according to a thought. We must realize that it is impossible to have a thought without having a feeling about it and vice versa. They are inseparable.

Note that EVE is made of ADAM'S RIB. This is a clue to the

mystery of the soul's evolution that should not be missed. A RIB is curved and this reminds us that experience on the outer manifest level must move on a curve and not on a straight line since all experience must adhere to the same spherical movement that has been established on the higher levels of creation. Science shows us that energy does not move on a straight line but on continuous curves or waves.

Think about it for a moment. Suppose you cut your finger. If energy moved only forward, as it healed it would extend itself indefinitely, but instead it rebuilds and regenerates itself in rotating circles of energy that serve to restore the injured tissue. This continuing circle of energy assures the return of Life and Substance to their original point of being from all levels of their expression. This truth should encourage us not to be too upset by appearances and conditions that occur on this manifest level of experience, but to become non-resistant to the ever changing conditions that we see, knowing that all will be well even though we cannot yet comprehend what that will be.

Our story has brought us to the point where Substance is going to become a human body. Let's pause here and consider the possibility that this pure and perfect Substance, which manifests as a human body limited by its atomic condition, can eventually regain its freedom to express as purity and perfection. This idea that the body can take on perfection seems to be a difficult one for most people to accept. The human race has associated body only with the earthly experience and considers it doomed forever to decay and dissolution. On the other hand, people are not as resistant to the idea that it is possible for an individual to attain mental illumination or so-called self-realization. Restoring consciousness from its state of ignorance to enlightenment is an accepted idea in many metaphysical circles and religions, but most fail to realize that the mental and physical are inseparable. What happens in consciousness must also happen in body!

The creation story reveals that the Life idea and the Substance idea (HEAVEN AND EARTH), which descended to the lower manifest sphere of activity, both undergo refinement and ascend to the higher levels. The return in consciousness makes ascension of the body possible and the experience of death unnecessary. Just as the mental nature ascends to a higher perspective, so too, must the body ascend to higher expression since mind and body are inseparable.

If this was not Cosmic law, Jesus would not have been able to ascend His body into a higher sphere of activity. Everyone and everything in the universe must comply with the same universal law that has been established from the BEGINNING. The same law of transformation of body that was available to Jesus is available to all, once it is understood. Since the two ideas in MIND are attached and inseparable as part of the triune Principle, both Life and Substance must follow the same descending and ascending process. If one returns, the other must also return. Whether or not we fully understand this law does not change it. One must be willing to let go of former concepts, particularly religious ones that bind the thinking processes, in order to learn new Truth.

[See Figure 16]

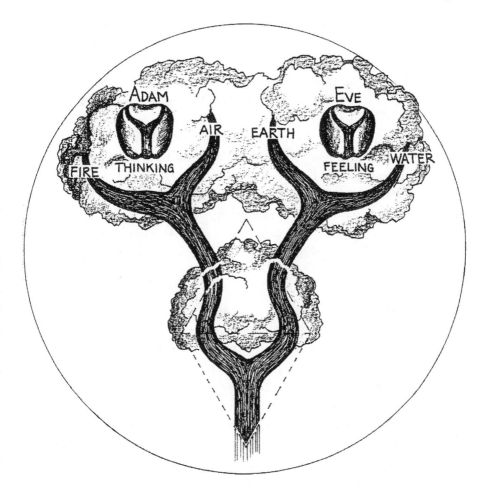

Figure #16

FRUITS OF THE TREES

Once again we can use our imaging power and recall the symbolic TREES in the GARDEN. Now we can place ADAM and EVE in that image as illustrated here.

They are the fruit of the TREES. They each have within them the whole, perfect pattern of the TREE. This is because the self-reflective nature of the Absolute Whole always reproduces a holographic image of Itself. Therefore, no matter how many times the image will be divided into separate pieces, each piece will contain the whole.

79

Could this be the answer to that puzzling question about death? I had never forgotten the secret given to me when I was nine years old. "People are not supposed to die; it is not God's way." Genesis states that MIND and body cannot be separated. It became clear to me that what I held in MIND would appear. If a physical existence in a physical, material world was what I could imagine for myself, then that is why I have a material, physical body and live in a world composed of atoms. Genesis also says that the Perfect Idea of Life descends and then it also ascends. Was it time for me to imagine a different kind of existence for myself? According to scripture, there will be a constant progression from one level of MIND to another. Or should I say change of orbit? Is this the way to avoid death? I had to read on.

Scientists discovered the holograms that had been shattered into many pieces contain the whole original image in each piece. This is not a mystery to those who understand the Genesis story. We know that the original whole and perfect pattern of Life and Substance is in each reflected image. Therefore, there is more to a human being than we have been taught.

Now it is time for us to use our scientific perspective and consider a holographic image. A hologram can be defined as an interference pattern of light waves on a photographic plate. This image can be seen in space as a three dimensional form. Without getting too technical, scientists know that it takes two amplified waves of energy interacting with each other to produce a modulating frequency. This is the "beat" or "rhythm" of the two combined opposing waves. We should not be surprised that two opposite waves interfering with each other produces the "beat." They are the same two original forces of the GOD SEED!

Scientists concluded that it is this interference pattern of vibrating waves that stores the information needed to produce a holographic image. This image will appear to be real and three dimensional even though in fact it is not.

In order to produce a hologram, they need two light beams, each vibrating at a different "beat" or "rhythm." A laser light is used because it stays at one frequency over long distances. It does not spread out like the beam from a flashlight but stays narrowly focused. The laser light is passed through a half mirror shaped like a triangle which splits it, sending it in two different directions. The first beam is called the reference beam. It is passed through a lens and then projected onto a photographic plate that bears an imprinted image. The other beam is called the working beam and it is projected onto another mirror which reflects it through a lens onto yet another mirror to project the image into space.

This sounds familiar! If we look at this process we see that it compares favorably with the Genesis story. We have seen one LIGHT split in two directions and a progression of that LIGHT through mirrored reflections. The result is that an IMAGE and LIKENESS is produced (Cosmic Christ). That IMAGE is reflected again and becomes a LIVING SOUL. This reflection can be reproduced again as many individual souls.

Scientists also discovered that holograms, which are Substance. is in each reflected image. Therefore, there is more to a human being than we have been taught.

Could each of us be a holographic image that is being projected in space-time from the original IMAGE and LIKENESS, the Cosmic Christ which is outside of space-time? When Life and Substance reach the lower level (vibrating "beat") it can be formed and shaped according to the original pattern that has been created. The projected image is three dimensional and appears to be real, but could it be that it is really only a reflection of the real "us" and we believe what we see is real? Perhaps the part of us that we don't see is reality and not the part of us that we see at this level of atomic matter. This hypothesis merits scrutiny.

Another fascinating point of all this is that medical researchers now know that each cell in our bodies carries all the information required to make an additional copy. They know how to take a cell from an organ of the body and electrically stimulate it into activity so that it will grow and reproduce itself as a new organ. Of course, this breakthrough will help keep the physical body alive longer and thus help us in our evolutionary journey toward the full awakening to who and what we really are.

I didn't see the hologram principle in Genesis when the

first revelations came to me. I didn't know anything about holograms. It would be many years before I read about them. Then it became another affirmation of the laws I had found in the creation story! Here we can link together the Quantum Theory with the Hologram and see how what we DECIDE to see is what will appear. However, it will actually be an illusion.

Now I invite you to use your image-making ability to see the way holograms work. Get an image of the original triangle we found in the first line of the Bible. Now see its reflection super imposed upside down over it, making the six-pointed star. Now pass the light from these through the lens of your consciousness and see the original triad repeated again, this time appearing below the original star.

Next, see its light making another triad, but this time it is inverted with its apex at the bottom. It is attached to the preceding triad. See the triads repeated in this same way again and again forming a chain of upright and upside down triangles. The line that connects them can be traced over each set of triangles, looking like figure "X's' or "8's."

This is the way energy flows from the invisible to the visible and also through the spine of the human body. The medical symbol of the Caduceus also illustrates this flow of intertwining energy. A serpent is used to represent this flowing energy current. This image will help you understand what is now going to happen in our story.

The Creation Story has taken us to the point where the GOD SEED has reproduced and multiplied and is now ready to become individualized and material. Everything is ready for the manifestation of a material body but one essential act must still take place before materialism can be experienced. The individualized soul must volunteer for the experience! Only those who choose to experience Life and Substance in the outer sphere will be given the privilege.

One might wonder if material existence a privilege. Sometimes it does seem to be when it becomes a very difficult experience. It is a privilege because those who volunteer for the experience of becoming material beings are admitted into the Cosmic School that trains Co-creators. Yes, going to school is difficult, yet it is a privilege because the rewards are great and it is the necessary preparation for greater activities that require more responsibility. The soul must enroll for this course of instruction and it is rigorous, but those who graduate from the earthly school receive the "Master Degree." They will have the privilege of becoming a Master of all they survey and the struggle and hardship will have been worth it.

Genesis II explains how this choice between staying in the inner spheres, or manifesting on the outer perimeter, is presented to the soul with the introduction of a SERPENT.

NOW THE SERPENT WAS MORE SUBTLE THAN ANY BEAST OF THE FIELD WHICH THE LORD GOD HAD MADE.

The SERPENT is simply the original movement of GOD Breath that we found in the first Chapter of Genesis. This movement was next called RIVER on the higher level. The word SERPENT is now used to represent this same currant of energy and impulse that is still moving as the soul approaches the threshold of the outer manifest realm. The characteristically sluggish, undulating movements of a SERPENT depict the nature of thought and feeling. They are SUBTLE, that is, they are hardly noticed by the individualized self. Is there anything more subtle than thinking and feeling?

The SERPENT is the ever present urge to experience Life and is found in the FIELD. This FIELD is the field of electrical thought and feeling energy (ADAM and EVE). The intention (will) of the GOD SEED is to experience Its Life and Substance on all levels of Mind and even on its outmost perimeter. This seventh level is the outer realm where experience will be more difficult than on the inner realms because Life and Substance will have been extended to the outermost point for expansion. Therefore, this energy must turn back upon itself and incrustation will occur, causing a crystallization of both consciousness and form.

This will temporarily entrap the soul because now there is a barrier between the lower bodies and the higher original pattern of self. This barrier must be broken through and will be the challenge for the soul.

This is why the soul must volunteer. The MOVING of the SPIRIT OF GOD is still acting, but now as thought and feeling. Its movement is SUBTLE. At this stage it is called the SERPENT and it speaks to EVE:

AND HE SAID UNTO THE WOMAN, YEA, THAT GOD SAID, YE SHALL NOT EAT OF EVERY TREE OF THE GARDEN?

Why is the question put to EVE and not to ADAM? EVE hears the question because as already discussed, when the polar energies passed through the "lens" of the FIRMAMENT on the higher level, the first point of attention in Mind shifted from the idea of Life to the idea of Substance because the TRIANGLE inverted. This same Substance is now called EVE and it is through this feeling aspect that experience in matter will begin. The driving force behind experience will be feelings of desire. Since desire is linked with thought, the soul inwardly knows a price must be paid for experience in the outer realm and these words in the Bible make that clear:

AND THE WOMAN SAID UNTO THE SERPENT: WE MAY EAT OF THE FRUIT OF THE TREES OF THE GARDEN, BUT OF THE FRUIT OF THE TREE WHICH IS IN THE MIDST OF THE GARDEN, GOD HATH SAID, YE SHALL NOT EAT OF IT, NEIGHER SHALL YE TOUCH IT, LEST YE DIE.

When this passage is read carefully, it is clear that eating from the TREE is not forbidden. The decree from on high is that it is not to be eaten LEST (unless) one is willing to DIE. DIE to what? Since no physical body has yet been produced and all of this is taking place in Mind, the soul can only DIE to a state of consciousness. The price for experiencing KNOWLEDGE OF GOOD AND EVIL on the material level means one must DIE to the realization of the soul's true identity, the perfect Life idea.

Remember the rule that has already been established? "That which is to be must come from that which already is." In other words, something cannot be made from nothing, so the state of consciousness that "knows" whole Life must DIE (be sacrificed) so that "knowing about" Life can be born on the atomic level of manifestation. The emotional nature is tantalized by the pulsating currents of energy in GARDEN of Mind and the desire to experience life in a tangible way becomes the focus of attention. Entering into the realm of materialism is serious business and it is not forced upon the soul! It must be chosen through free will! Death of the higher states of consciousness will occur when the soul enters a physical body.

One might ask, "Why does this have to happen?" The GOD SEED must experience Life and Substance on the manifest level so that it can fulfill its original purpose, to unite HEAVEN AND EARTH! Earlier we saw that it is possible for EARTH to receive HEAVEN and the impulse of the SPIRIT OF GOD is always MOVING toward that goal. We see that pulsating movement now as the SERPENT tempting EVE. Souls are needed to bring the GOD SEED energy into the outer realm and to radiate the higher consciousness through all matter so that it may be purified and lifted up into perfected forms. The soul recognizes the cost entailed in this service to the scheme of evolution. Since the SERPENT is not the soul's enemy, nor is it Satan who lures the soul into disobedience, it reassures EVE of the continuance of Life and that reward will come if such a sacrifice is made:

YE SHALL NOT SURELY DIE, FOR GOD DOTH KNOW THAT IN THE DAY YE EAT THEREOF, THEN YOUR EYES SHALL BE OPENED, AND YE SHALL BE AS GODS KNOWING BOTH GOOD AND EVIL.

This dialogue is not taking place between two different entities. Remember everything is happening within Mind. After individualization is realized the natural Life impulse to experience (SERPENT) impresses the scheme for evolution upon the soul. What sounds like a conversation between two parties is the inherent polarity within the soul that is presenting contrasts at this level of creation. The opportunity presented to the individualizing living soul is to BE AS GODS, KNOWING BOTH GOOD AND EVIL. What does that mean? It means participation in the fullness of experience!

Let us consider the nature of the KNOWING BOTH GOOD AND EVIL. GOOD and EVIL are the contrasting polarities of the outer level.

There, the two original forces appear to oppose each other and produce conflict on the material plane. However, this is not reality. At the GOD SEED level of consciousness there is no conflict. These forces, which operate with perfect equilibrium, bring about the manifestation of Life and Substance. However, on the manifest level there is friction between the two and this friction will cause continual self-reflection in the soul and the result will be constant changes as different viewpoints in consciousness take place. This will be the progressive states and stages of evolution as mankind moves from ignorance to enlightenment. Therefore, in reality one force is not GOOD and the other EVIL, but both are necessary for evolution.

The soul will be unable to discern the true nature of these forces and will have only KNOWLEDGE about them. Knowledge is the accumulation of facts that appear to be true in space-time and is not truth, but only knowledge about the truth. Please note that the FRUIT "eaten" is not from the TREE OF GOOD AND EVIL but instead from the TREE OF KNOWLEDGE OF GOOD AND EVIL. In other words, in truth there is no GOOD and EVIL, there is only GOD, or universal giving. In fact nothing that appears on the manifest level can be all GOOD or all EVIL, since both contain some of each other, just as in the Yin/Yang principle. From human sense, things are seen from a particular perspective which is limited and conditioned by consciousness and little of what really is occurring is known. This limited condition is only temporary but will take a long time to blossom into full awareness of the truth of things.

Our story illustrates that the proposal to appropriate opposites in consciousness is filtered through the thinking and feeling mechanism. Just as we think and feel about things today, so too, did we do the same at the soul level before we chose to come into embodiment as a material being. The thinking went something like this:

THE TREE WAS GOOD FOR FOOD, AND THAT IT WAS PLEASANT TO THE EYES, AND A TREE TO BE DESIRED TO MAKE ONE WISE, SHE TOOK OF THE FRUIT THEREOF, AND DID EAT, AND GAVE ALSO UNTO HER HUSBAND WITH HER, AND HE DID EAT.

The feeling, emotional nature of the soul is driven by the Will of GOD (SERPENT), which acts as a catalyst at this level of creation. This Will is the stimulus to know contrasts and gain true understanding of all things of creation, even on its outer perimeter. It is this impulse to unite HEAVEN AND EARTH that pushes the soul to temporarily sacrifice its own well-being and take on the consciousness of KNOWLEDGE, rather than actually "knowing" Life and Substance.

Inherent in the soul, is the urge to give itself away and that is why it is able to make this choice. Individualized free will must be exercised and here is an essential truth. The soul feels that it is GOOD to use its individual free will. Indeed, without contrasts, or opposites, there would be no need for free will and it is only through making choices on the outer realm of expression that the intention to build a permanent temple for the GOD SEED can be carried out. Through right choices purification and perfection will come, therefore, there must be an opportunity to make choices. Wisdom is the mental quality necessary along with the feeling quality of love that is essential to become a Co-creator with GOD. After the choice is made to BE AS GODS, the KNOWLEDGE of contrasting images is appropriated into consciousness. Then something occurs that ushers the soul into the manifest level:

AND THE EYES OF THEM BOTH WERE OPENED, AND THEY KNEW THAT THEY WERE NAKED.

This symbolism indicates that the consequence of the sacrifice is an awareness of being NAKED. In other words, there is now a lack of understanding concerning the truth of being. The EYES of thinking and feeling (THEM BOTH) are directed, or OPENED, to the outer plane and ignorance about the inner planes prevails. A simple way to think of this is that now the attention of thought and feeling is directed from within to what will appear without. An actual separation occurs between the higher mental nature, which remains on the invisible plane, and the feeling nature, which will appear as visible manifest substance, or atomic matter.

The mental nature (ADAM) is also "atom." This is the permanent atom of the soul on this level. Its nature is to radiate and magnetize mental electrical energy. This activity simultaneously occurs on the manifest level as atoms draw other atoms to build a physical body. Since the mental nature and the feeling nature are really inseparable, they function as one, but only the material body is visible to the outer sense nature. However, the GOD Intelligence, as the perfect holographic pattern for body, is in every atom of the body and will be reproduced in every cell. The GOD SEED reproduces through the hologram principle, so that the whole is always present in that which appears to be only a part of the whole and apart from the whole.

AND ADAM AND HIS WIFE HID THEMSELVES FROM THE PRESENCE OF THE LORD GOD AMONGST THE TREES OF THE GARDEN.

The Bible explains that the result of this choice is fear. Ignorance of truth (being NAKED) causes thought and feeling to experience fear and they hide from the LORD GOD. The LORD GOD is really the law of our own being but thought and feeling are ignorant about that. Contact with the LORD GOD is experienced through the activity of Mind, but at this low vibratory rate the soul does not know or understand the LORD (law) which now seems oppressive. In other words, the lower mental and emotional nature of the soul that now resides on the manifest plane, "hides" by becoming engrossed in the sensations of the body (TREES OF THE GARDEN) and because of ignorance, fearfully denies contact with its true GOD nature. Fear now becomes a great barrier between the soul and its true self that can act only as law and is not visible to the physical being

I WILL GREATLY MULTIPLY YOUR PAIN IN CHILDBEARING; IN PAIN YE SHALL BRING FORTH CHILDREN; YET YOUR DESIRE SHALL BE FOR YOUR HUSBAND AND HE SHALL RULE OVER YE.

This is not an indictment against women. Nor is it punishment, but a statement as to how the LORD (law) must work on the manifest level. The "woman" in the story is EVE and we know that she represents the emotional, feeling nature. It is through this aspect of our being that we shall BRING FORTH new experiences and new forms, which are called CHILDREN in this passage. With them will come pain because newness and change is difficult. It often brings great emotional trauma but our DESIRE yearns to mate with our HUSBAND, which is thought (ADAM). This has to be so because the original principle has the intention of union between the two. The moment the initial separation of the One force occurred, the desire for harmonious union between the two opposites came into existence and now this same DESIRE is experienced on the manifest level. In other words, the emotional nature will desire a mental understanding of what happens. The law (LORD) decrees that there will be suffering with every new birth of new experiences, new forms, and even new perspectives. These are the CHILDREN. Because each new stage of development requires some sacrifice of what already is being experienced, this brings emotional PAIN. Each new birth, however, helps to awaken the soul.

The HUSBAND WILL RULE OVER the desire nature since the HUSBAND is the mental nature and nothing can be brought forth without an initial thought. Experience will be governed by the nature of the ruling thought in consciousness.

IN THE SWEAT OF THY FACE THOU SHALL EAT BREAD.

On the material level, the sleepy state of ADAM, our mental nature, produces confusing and uncomfortable conditions. Sustenance will have to come by the SWEAT OF THY FACE. You may remember the FACE is a derivative of the "sur-face" and is a symbol for the ability to recognize. When recognition of self is confined to only this outer level of being, life is tedious and the soul has to SWEAT it out. Since life will be seen by the outer appearances only, the mental nature will misunderstand what is seen. There will be constant effort to solve problems from the same level upon which they occur and this will be a laborious and futile task. Things will seem to change but unless a higher perspective is brought into them, they will only be shifted from one place to another, or appear in one form or another. This will make life difficult. Nothing will be known about how to manifest things through the power of thought and the spoken word so everything will have to be made with the physical realm limitations.

As difficult as this all seems, it is nevertheless necessary and adheres to the original law of sacrifice made at the highest level. "As above, so below." This is the only way that a Co-creator with GOD can be produced. Scripture shows that according to Cosmic law it is only after free will has been exercised that the Co-creating course of instruction begins and the material body condition manifests. Genesis describes this manifestation in this way:

UNTO ADAM ALSO AND TO HIS WIFE DID THE LORD GOD MAKE COATS OF SKIN AND CLOTHED THEM.

With this statement we see that progressive self-reflection has caused the GOD SEED to take on material form. The COATS OF SKIN signify that Substance has reached the material body condition. The Christ Self or LIVING SOUL can now think and feel through many bodies of material substance. Through this process Its individualized feeling (EVE) and thought (ADAM) will one day become WISE and BE AS GODS. Herein is GOD'S purpose and plan. Through this subtle urge to experience, or act out thoughts about life on a material level, wisdom and right action (love) will be expressed by the souls (individual Christs).

All the while, the curve of evolution will gradually return the diminished awareness of Life and the vibration of Substance to their higher frequency and perfect condition. That which temporarily feels empty and seeks to be filled will eventually be filled. This is the "fulfillment of the law" referred to by Jesus Christ. Human beings are designed to be the Co-creators with GOD, but only through constant choice. Throughout evolution the lower mental nature of every individual gradually awakens from the DEEP SLEEP as choices are made and eventually the soul becomes totally aware of its Christ Self nature. Through this gradual awakening, the material, feeling body is also refined and perfected so that it may become the permanent temple the living GOD.

To eat from the TREE OF KNOWLEDGE OF GOOD AND EVIL means choosing to experience life in an electrical force field that relates to experience only through the five senses. Remember, the system was set up with the number seven. Two of the seven senses will not function on the outer plane until much experience has been gained. The five senses of touch, taste, smell, hearing, and sight operate on the outer plane and they report the natural polarity of creation to the brain. Because this reporting is very limited it produces mirrored images from the Mind which are also very limited and off balance. The human being ("hu" meaning humus or earth) will not realize that what is being sensed is just a mirrored image that is very limited and is only a surface view of Life and Substance.

[See Figure 17]

[See Figure 18]

Figure #17

THE TWO TREES SEPARATE

The full, complete life is symbolized as the TREE OF LIFE. It reflects our perfect pattern, the Cosmic Christ. This TREE can be "known" through ADAM, the mental nature. It can also be "felt" through EVE, the feeling nature. However, with only five senses operating, the lower mental and feeling nature does not perceive the true wholeness of Life (TREE OF LIFE). Only a very restricted degree of Life and Substance is now being realized and experienced at the material level. This limitation is sensed as a definite separation, which in turn, causes a rupture in consciousness, resulting in an actual separation of the TWO TREES.

The tree that is the perfect pattern (TREE OF LIFE) remains on the inner, invisible level of Mind and the tree that perceives contrasts (TREE OF KNOWLEDGE OF GOOD AND EVIL) manifests as atomic material on the outer level. This matter takes the form of the pattern that is within the atoms and become a human, physical body that very much resembles a tree!

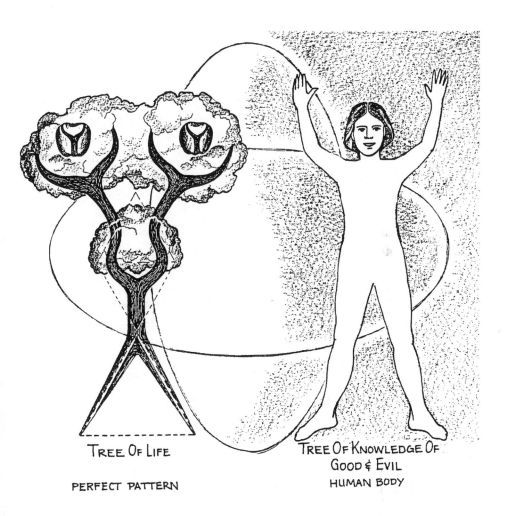

TREE OF LIFE

PERFECT PATTERN

TREE OF KNOWLEDGE OF
GOOD & EVIL

HUMAN BODY

Figure #18

THE MYSTICAL MARRIAGE

This illustration presents the TRIANGLE (trinity) of energy in a new way. At its apex is the individualized Christ Self, which is directly connected to the Cosmic Christ at a higher level. This individualized Christ Self holds the idea of perfect body and complete illumination in consciousness at all times while the material body-brain seeks satisfaction in the outer manifest realm.

The TWO TREES stem from the original ideas CREATED by GOD in the first line of the Bible when they were labeled HEAVEN AND EARTH.

At the manifest level the expression, HEAVEN AND EARTH appear to be separate, but in reality this cannot be true since they are both part of a trinity. The limitations of the five senses cause the illusion of separateness to exist in consciousness.

Because of this there is a feeling of lack and of a need for fulfillment. This is why the soul seeks union with someone or something in the outer realm to alleviate its feeling of emptiness and loneliness. This continual seeking does not satisfy the soul until ultimately there is a union in consciousness between all three aspects of the self. This eventual union is assured by the character of the inner Principle and constitutes what is called the mystical marriage.

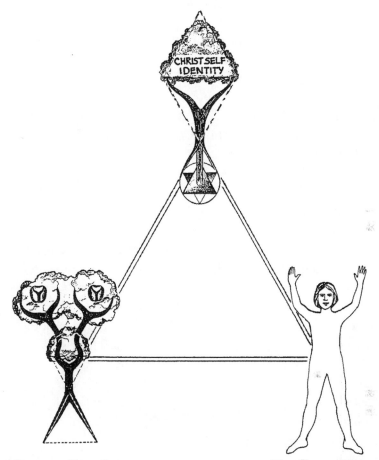

THE PERFECT BODY PATTERN   THE FLESH BODY
                                          IN HUMAN EXPERIENCE

The Christ Self is directly connected to its material body, which is Its lower mental and emotional mechanism. There cannot be complete fulfillment until a threefold union in consciousness is achieved. Eventually, through the process of evolution and gradual awakening to the Christ identity, a higher level of being will be realized. That union is a level of experience that has been called the "Kingdom of Heaven" which is the connecting point with the original permanent atom. Remember, the FIRMAMENT produced the permanent atom, which in turn produced the Cosmic Christ. All are at the same level of Mind. Realization of the truth brings conscious union between the bride (bodies of substance, physical, mental, and emotional) and the bridegroom (the Christ Self, or LIVING SOUL), which is directly connected with the Cosmic level of awareness. Such is the mystical marriage referred to in the Bible.

Countless myths, legends, and fairy tales have been written around this theme wherein symbolic characters are used to illustrate the individualized Christ Self or so-called Higher Self and Its lower bodies. Preparation and progression in consciousness toward the mystical marriage reveals that everything happens within us even though it appears to be outside of us. How is this possible? It is so because everything is an inverted mirrored image of that which is held in consciousness.

In the grand creative process we are really a Principle of Mind and all things happen within that Mind. The only reality is consciousness! Therefore, there are infinite possibilities to know and to experience.

What will we know and experience tomorrow, or a million years from now, or a million years beyond that? What will we be? The only thing we can be certain about as we look at the plan from our present limited view, is that there cannot be an end to "knowing" and "being." We move from one stage of development to another and since everything is happening within spheres that return again and again as they rotate, there really is no beginning or end, just as there are no beginnings and ending in the Infinite. This is why Truth seems to be such a mystery as we delve into its many layers.

Can you believe it? All this has only taken us through Chapter III of Genesis! How many evenings it took me to realize what was contained in just a few pages of the Bible I

don't recall, but it flowed easily and was like eating popcorn and watching a movie. Each line presented a new image and it was the greatest adventure of my life! The days that followed were so filled with joy that I cried at the least little thing. The tears were those of joy, not sadness. Everything seemed so wonderful, I felt free and "lifted up" in all I did and I loved everyone.

Looking back, I now realize that my emotional body was going through a cleansing and adjustment process as I was being enfolded in the love of my Higher Self. I had made contact with the invisible me. Because I had listened and followed my inner instructions I would never be the same as I was before. This quickened my desire to know more about life and yes, even death. I wanted to know the whole Plan God held in MIND for humanity, so I had to continue my reading sessions as often as possible. They were a blessing to me.

At the same time this was happening, I was attending to my duties as Spiritual leader at the Methodist Women's Society. I made an announcement for one of the women there. She needed volunteers to help with her brain-injured child and I decided to help. That would be a significant turning point in my life that I am sure was connected to my discovery in Genesis. My first session with her and her son brought good news to me.

Since we both were involved in Church work, our conversation naturally turned to spiritual things. She began telling me that she believed that Christ was in all of us and that we all had the potential to know that we were a Christ. My heart leaped with joy! I told her that I believed that too. "Where did you hear that Christ is in you?" I asked. "I go to a Unity Church on Wednesday nights and that is their teaching." She said it was a metaphysical church, but the word metaphysical was unknown to me. She explained that it was an interpretation of Scripture that went deeper than the traditional church. It was known as New Thought, which explained the symbols in the Bible. How much more did I need to hear? Not a thing!

I made arrangements to go with her the coming Wednesday.

After the Service they had classes to attend. I chose one that was led by a newly Ordained Minister of Unity and resolved to continue to study with her. Surely, she had been presented to me because I was ready to know more. She told me about a Unity correspondence course that I could take by mail, which I started immediately and sent in my papers to be graded on a regular basis. All this was an answer to my prayers and I was so thankful to my inner voice for bringing it all about. It seemed reasonable that what I held in my mind was bearing fruit because this was the way the Law of MIND worked.

Chapter 5

SOUND WAVES PRODUCE
THE DOUBLE HELIX

Now that atomic material has come into our story, one might wonder what will happen to the manifested Life in the GOD SEED as it goes through experience on the atomic level. There are a series of stories that follow the creation story in Genesis and we will explore them in this chapter. They illustrate particular stages of development that became possible when certain required conditions of evolution had been met according to universal laws. Some stories in the Bible are pure allegories, such as the one about ADAM and EVE and the ones that immediately follow are also pure allegories. However, before we review what they have to teach us, let's pause to align ourselves with what we now know about Genesis and what science is presenting to us in our time.

THE DOUBLE HELIX

In 1953, two scientists named James Watson and Frances Crick, discovered the "double helix" which they called the "secret of life" and built the structure of DNA. For this they were awarded the Nobel Prize. We can find that "double helix" and DNA structure in Genesis I. Actually the first line of the Bible holds the key to the "secret of life."

Proceeding from the word BEGINNING and following the progressive repetition of the words AND GOD SAID in this first chapter of the Bible, we see a series of triangles being produced out of the original triangle of energy. This happens because GOD CREATED interaction between two different frequencies of energy. One actively initiates (radiation) and the other passively receives (magnetism). Thus, a mirrored and inverted image of the original triangle is the result and it can continue to reproduce over and over again. Since the nature of this moving energy is vibration, its MOVEMENT produces vibrating sound and the Bible tells us that it is this sound that brings forth triune images.

Our clue to this process is the phrase AND GOD SAID. These words are many times repeated in Genesis I, each time producing two trinities of energy. Each is a mirrored inverted image of the proceeding one. We can picture these triangular images with the apex of each connecting with the other, one at the top and one at the bottom so that they form an "X." This is the same image as the "double helix" discovered by Watson and Crick. Four of these "X" patterns appear in Genesis I. If we place them one on top of the other as they flow out of the original triangle we have a chain of eight making four "X's."

X

X

X

X

This chain of inverted triangles looks very much like the DNA structure made by Watson and Crick but it appears stiff with sharp corners in comparison. Here is where we can use our imagination and put these triangles in motion in order to change the appearance of this chain. The word "helix" means swirling, rolling, spiraling like a corkscrew. The Genesis ladder of "X" components is really vibrating energy, which when interacting, swirl, roll, and spiral like a corkscrew. Imagining this motion, we can see the sharp corners disappearing and a spiral of energy swirling round and round. Now our scriptural model looks like the DNA, "secret of life" model of Watson and Crick.

Another fascinating point is that when the scientists separated the two strands of this "double helix," they found that it made a copy of itself and once again become two. We should not be amazed by this, since we know that GOD CREATED a perfect system of reproduction through Self-reflected, mirror images and each image copies the whole, complete pattern of the original. This same reproductive process can be seen in every cell of our bodies. When one becomes two, each holds the whole pattern so that the making of copies can continue.

SOUND VIBRATION

Because scripture uses the words, AND GOD SAID, again and again in this Creation story, it should alert us to the fact that sound waves play an important part in creating forms. The importance of sound waves must not escape our attention here. If we want to draw a picture of a wave we would not draw a straight horizontal line. Instead, we would draw a line that has peaks and valleys, indicating a wave motion. If we place a triangle inside the first peak of this line (its apex at the top) and then place an inverted triangle (its apex at the bottom) in the valley that follows the peak, we have two triangles side by side. If we continue this pattern with a series of triangles, inverting every other one, we can see how these alternating triangles, which are currents of energy, produce a wave effect.

Simple scientific demonstrations show us that sound waves cause particles to aggregate into patterns, which is analogous to atoms aggregating into three dimensional patterns. In other words, sound waves make orderly patterns. Now we see why the Genesis writer continually uses the phrase AND GOD SAID.

According to the creation story of the Bible sound waves are actually in atomic matter! They can be traced back to IN THE BEGINNING when the one frequency became two frequencies. Science observes these two frequencies as "standing waves" and they call the intervals of rest between them "nodes." This continual movement and rest cause wavelets or circles of energy wave patterns that cross over each other to create complex vibrating patterns. These wave patterns interfering and intermingling with each other leave the total of all the impressions in the stuff of Substance so that the whole is recorded in each pattern. What would seem to be separate and independent still remains whole because of this ability to cross pattern.

This is the way Divine Intelligence of the Whole is preserved in all of creation. It is also the way an idea impressed upon Substance can be shared by the whole of humanity. Information is stored by the interaction of the wave frequencies. Not only is it stored, it is contained in every particle. No matter how fragmented, the whole pattern is in each fragment. So, we see that a particle which is a basic building block for matter contains the whole original pattern of Life and it is continually being impressed upon Substance which gives it form. This principle is demonstrated in holograms as discussed in the last chapter. Scientists have seen evidence that our brains store information, as does a hologram, and some believe that we have a genetic code in our chromosomes. Actually, every cell in the human body has all the information needed to make a copy of the body or any body part. What a wonderful system or creation GOD has wrought, we need only to awaken to the possibilities that exist for us!

It seems the writer of Genesis is telling us that the moving energy currents which produce sound waves play a continuous part in creation. If this is true on the higher, inner spheres of creation it has to be true also on the lower, outer sphere since there is only one law that operates in all spheres and on all levels. Jesus says, in the Book of Thomas, a book not included in the Bible, "I know Spirit as a movement and rest within me." If everything is affected by the movement and rest of vibrations, this should give us pause when we think about the sounds that are produced by the human race in the physical world. What sounds are productive and what sounds are destructive? Indeed, what words enhance the universal plan and what words hinder that plan? Each of us plays a part in the evolutionary plan. Where do we stand? Do we let the LIGHT pierce the DARKNESS or do we block that LIGHT?

FULFILLING THE LAW

The science of Genesis has presented us with a picture of flowing energy frequencies through triangular mirrored inverted images. Using words as symbols, we are shown that each formation of an "X" pattern indicates a stepping down of the vibrating energy patterns until they reach the place where they can form the perfect MAN, the Cosmic Christ. Then, as a LIVING SOUL (realization of "I AM") this MAN can reproduce into many souls, each containing a replica of the original structure of "X" patterns and each realizing "I AM."

This structure of life revealed in Genesis is the "secret of life." It shows the origin of our beingness and the process of involution as Spirit involves Itself in matter. From the establishment of this creative law, we have seen how evolution begins and human beings eventually appear upon the face of the planet Earth. How many million, or billions of years did it take to produce material bodies of intelligent life as we know it today? Not even the scientists can be sure of that, but there is no doubt that what we see existing in time-space took so much time that it is incalculable from our present knowledge. The Bible says that GOD'S time is not our time and that is surely so! The beauty of it all is that we are still evolving!

How much time will it take for us to reproduce our Perfect Christ Pattern, the mirrored image that is hidden within us? We cannot say, but we can be sure that we are progressing toward full understanding and expression. We can believe this because we have seen this unalterable law established in Genesis. Just as cannot see the oak tree in the acorn, or the chicken inside the broken eggshell, we know its complete pattern is there to be reproduced when right conditions are met.

What else has the creation story of the Bible revealed to us? Certainly, it has presented very impressive laws for us to understand and to live by. When we act or even think against the natural flow of currents CREATED by GOD we suffer, so it is well that we learn these laws and abide by them and trust in them. This is because these flowing currents of energy make up our own true nature. Imbalanced energy causes "dis-ease" that is experienced in body and mind. Genesis I is a gold mine full of nuggets called laws and it has yielded many nuggets as a result of our "digging" for them. Here are some basic essentials for living a harmonious and balanced life:

1. Daily awareness that we live, move, and have being in Mind.
2. Suffering comes when we do not reflect God's nature.
3. God's energy is continuous, constant, and everywhere present.
4. There is polarity in all things; learn to see this.
5. Self-reflection is the "motor" for involution and evolution.
6. Our thoughts manifest as reflected images and experiences.
7. God's acts through the creative laws.
8. Our "observation" reflects back to us what we "expect" to see.

9. Everything acts as "what goes around, comes around."
10. Life and Substance move in rotating cycles.
11. We only see part of the whole and appearances can be deceiving.
12. "I AM" identity causes a sense of separation from good.
13. This "need" forces choice, which is essential for evolution.
14. Since atoms of our bodies regenerate, we can too.
15. Change your mind, establish and image it, and then experience it.
16. There are continual new beginnings.
17. We are made of four elements: earth, water, air, fire.
18. We live in four worlds; physical, emotional, mental and spiritual.
19. What we think of ourselves affects everything in our life.
20. Newness must come from what already is and requires sacrifice.
21. Our "sleepy" mental nature is gradually awakening.
22. Our emotional nature should "balance" with our mental nature.
23. Thought and feeling are attached and cannot operate separately.
24. Every atom reflects our permanent atom.
25. We are not "born in sin" but chose earthly experience.
26. We work in energy fields to spiritualize atomic matter.
27. Fear, not GOD, is the cause of all pain and labor.
28. Sound power (spoken word) must be used intelligently.
29. Problems cannot be solved without changing perspective.
30. Through Self-reflection we change and progress in evolution.

DIMENSIONS AND LEVELS

The fundamental truth we have already learned from Genesis, which cannot be repeated too often, is that everything is MADE out of the TRIANGLE Principle. The way we use this Principle in everyday life is this:

What we think and feel about life will manifest

Simply put, whatever is known and believed about life is expressed in form, and experienced as situations, events and environment. This is the absolute law of the universe which cannot be made inoperative. It is always working! We have seen that this Principle assures manifestation and is the Cosmic guarantee that we will always have a body form. However, the body form is subject to the idea of Life that stands behind it. Underlying body is a field of intelligent energy. Therefore, bodies are really intelligences and it is helpful to think of all form in this way. Since the same Principle must operate in all dimensions of experience, we have to conclude that ideas of Life and Substance are also shaping forms (bodies) in every dimension.

So far illustrations in this book have shown how, on the lower levels of Mind, the triune Principle takes the form of a tree (a central trunk with two branches). This tree-shaped body form is manifested from the intelligence pattern of the three energy sources which is the TRIANGLE Principle Itself. The quality and appearance of the body conforms to the level of consciousness. The human level consciousness is dense; therefore, we have dense physical bodies. The body would naturally be different on the various levels since the degree and nature of intelligent awareness would differ in each of them. Since we are made of LIGHT and are the offspring of LIGHT, becoming the Sons of GOD might actually mean becoming Suns of GOD. Bodies at higher levels of awareness might appear as glowing or blazing LIGHT, such as recorded in the Gospels about the transfigured and ascended body of Jesus. The ramifications of this are not easily discerned by us at our present level of consciousness and we can only speculate what the possibilities might be.

However, it should now be clear that human beings have a level of awareness that manifests a flesh body, but in reality, they also exist in more than one level of intelligent activity at the same time in bodies that vibrate with a different rhythm. Why is it important to understand that there are other dimensions of Mind which are as yet generally beyond the belief system of human consciousness? It is important because once these realizations of other dimensions occur; simple logic can lead us to the possibility of communicating with higher levels of thought and even with Beings in other dimensions of intelligence than ourselves.

Down through history we have recorded experiences of many who claim to have made such contact. Is it all a fairy tale or is it possible? Even modern day science is discovering that there are more dimensions than the earth plane. According to Genesis, there are at least seven dimensions of consciousness, each having form, because we see them symbolically represented as the seven days of creation. Because the universe operates according to the law self-reflection, there are most likely seven mirrored images for every form. These are then reproduced seven times on seven levels, making forty nine images in all. This makes a very complex system of moving intelligent Life and Substance.

[see Figure #18-A]

Figure #18-A

A MULTI-DIMENSIONAL EXPRESSION

Since everything conforms to the basic TRIANGLE, these three aspects express on three planes, which are identified as the Cosmic Plane, the Solar Plane, and the Planetary Plane. Undoubtedly, in the great scheme of things, Beings are expressing themselves on each plane and in each dimension according to their capabilities.

These three Planes inter-penetrate with each other, being one, and yet being separate according to the particular planes of consciousness. Within all three, the Principle of three rules as it expands and contracts energy in circular, spiraling, spherical patterns, maintaining varied forms within every plane and dimension.

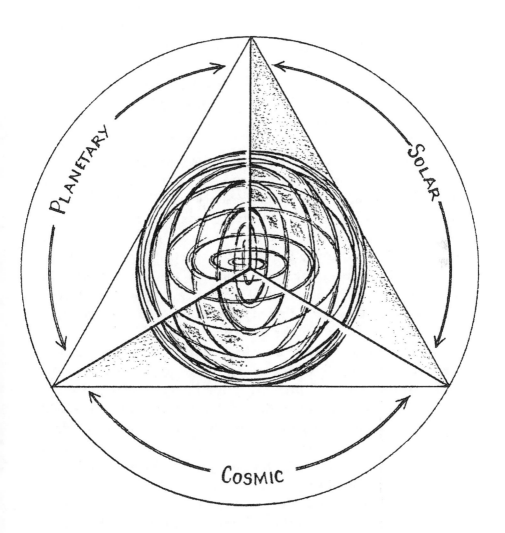

I feel I must express strongly to you the value that can be gained from these first few pages of Genesis. The wonderful little stories that follow are fun to decipher, but it will be helpful to review the laws I have compiled for you before continuing. See if you understand each point and why it is true. What we have discovered together, is difficult for many students, so don't be discouraged if some of it is still a muddle to you. It is a lot to grasp all at once.

Since I have been pondering this for over forty years, I am sure that every conclusion presented here did not come at my initial reading of Scripture. The essence was there, but through the wonderful law of self-reflection, more and more has been automatically revealed. The same process will work in you. Prove the law to yourself. See if it is true, that what dwells in your mind produces your experience. If you are interested in something and make it central in your consciousness, things will happen. Reviewing these laws when a problem arises will help you go above it and bring order in your life.

It certainly did in my life. As I continued to write lessons and also join a study group led by the Unity Minister, friends from my Methodist Church asked me to start a class for them because they heard me say things that interested them. I held a class in my home and soon after advertised in the local paper and gathered more students. A shopping center had made a room available to me at no cost. So began my sharing of metaphysical teachings.

During this period, dreams began to come that brought more light. I would awaken in the morning and then drop off into sleep again to experience vivid symbolic dreams. Sometimes they were about things in the world that were familiar, but other times they took place in the Cosmos. Often when I fully awakened, I knew I had been working out another secret that was hard to figure out.

All dreams are full of symbols. Some are prophetic and really do teach us about our destiny. Such was a dream that occurred many years ago and which I have shared only with a few others whom I felt would be interested. Since you are one of those, I will share it with you now.

I walked into a room and saw before me an opening about seven feet high and twelve feet wide. It was pitch black but I could see two pegs at the bottom, one on the right and one on the left, with ropes tied around them. They were the kind of pegs and ropes used on a boat dock. The ropes appeared to go down into the abyss of darkness. The amazing thing about this dream was the figure that stood to the right of this opening. I can only describe him as beautiful because every feature seemed so perfect and his skin had a radiant quality. He had soft, wavy brown hair, neatly groomed, and wore a navy blue suit. As he looked at me, I felt he understood everything about me, in fact more than I knew about myself. Without question, I felt He was there to help me.

I asked him, "Where do the ropes on the pegs go?" He replied. "It does not matter where they go, you are going to get on one of them and go where it will take you." I chuckled at this seeming preposterous thing! "Oh no, I won't, I can't do that. Besides, I have these bags of groceries!" I was carrying a large brown bag of groceries in each arm. With his gentle gaze he said, "No matter how much you argue about it, you are going to go." Suddenly, a wave of fear enveloped me, but just as it came, it left me. I put the groceries on the floor and walked toward the peg on the right side of the opening. I stooped and took hold of the rope with both hands and swung my foot around into the darkness. Then I was amazed, the opening was not a pit, there was a floor beneath me and I found myself firmly supported. At that moment a golden light surrounded me and I was filled with joy. As I looked out from where I had come, I saw lots of people, and I called to them, "Come; come into the golden light, it is wonderful." The dream ended.

A dream that was in vivid color and with such a great Being in it could not be ignored or forgotten. A few years later this same individual visited me in another profound dream. Both are as real to me today as they were those many years ago. When talking to my teacher about this first dream, she said it clearly meant that I was going to teaching the metaphysics I had been studying. That made sense, since I was already teaching. However, I would not understand the symbols in the dream until certain events took place in my life. In fact, the symbolic meaning was so astonishing that perhaps there are still things in the dream that I may yet to discover.

Knowing the law of consciousness helped me realize why my life drastically changed after that dream. I was able to meet those changes without fear of letting go of my present circumstances. My husband and I had enjoyed a happy marriage, but now we did not see things the same way. My discovery and then the study of metaphysics caused me to change my thinking about many old ideas and traditional viewpoints.

Our differing views had been drawing us apart. He was not interested in my newfound inspiration and my eagerness to share it with students. This was a troubling time for us because we no longer had the same goals. I did not want what he wanted and he could not understand what I wanted. I was making life difficult for him because he could not enter into my interests. He felt left out, but did not want to join me. We were no longer compatible as husband and wife. Our children were grown and it was time to begin a new phase in our lives. Although we still respected and cared for each other we could not see a future together and decided upon an amicable dissolution of our marriage of twenty-eight years. Together, we worked out things harmoniously and I am glad to say thirty-six years later, we are still friends.

After this, I knew what the bags of groceries symbolized in my dream. They were my security. I had to be willing to let go of the security of being married and cared for and also my financial security. In order to enter into this next phase of life, it was necessary for me to leave my home, family, friends, and financial security. I would have to learn new things about life. From a sheltered life, I entered into an unknown world. For one who had no advanced education or job skills, who had married very young and never had been on her own, this was an entirely new experience. However, it was obvious to me that

I had created this for myself out of my own desire to learn more about life and death and to teach it. New doors opened for me then and have continued to do so. The law of consciousness does not fail us.

More about this great law operating through the TRIANGLE as polarity is revealed in the next story of Genesis. Now we are introduced to two characters that represent two sides of our nature as we enter into our evolutionary development.

NOT DISOBEDIENCE BUT UNIVERSAL LAW

Genesis 1V presents CAIN and ABEL to represent the way life will work now that the TWO TREES have separated, one remaining outside of space-time and the other beginning to evolve in the material realm. ABEL corresponds to the inner TREE OF LIFE and CAIN to the outer TREE OF KNOWLEDGE OF GOOD AND EVIL. As we approach their story, it is beneficial to realize that the separation between the invisible higher Self and the visible higher self has not been caused by disobedience to GOD. It is simply the law of physics working itself out.

Energy vibrates at a different frequency in the outer realm than it does in the inner realms. The atomic matter of the body will gradually be raised in vibration as intelligent activity is expressed through it. Eventually the frequency of vibration will harmonize with that of the higher mental body which is the Christ Self of the individual. It is attached to the lower bodies (fields of energy) by a beam of LIGHT (Intelligent Life idea). It seems that at our present stage of evolution, the higher senses, the extra-sensatory perception (sixth) and the intuitive (seventh), are being stimulated in many individuals. More conscious use of these two senses permits greater contact with other planes of experience.

Throughout evolution Life and Substance on the outer level have been understood in the opposite way of their true nature. As already explained, this is because of the inversion of the original triad when Self-reflection began on the Absolute level of Mind. Since human beings are mirrored reflections, they are able to perceive from their reflected vantage point. Remember the Genesis writer has called this the UNDER of the FIRMAMENT. Because of this natural outworking of the law, humans have not been able to see the whole, enduring aspect of themselves. This flip-flop in the creative process causes everything to be seen backward, that is from a reflected image, rather than from its mental cause, the ABOVE vantage point. Seeing life only from the UNDER side is effectively illustrated in the story of the two brothers that follows.

CAIN AND ABEL

AND ADAM KNEW EVE, HIS WIFE, AND SHE CONCEIVED.

Note the word KNEW. This makes it clear that conception takes place in Mind before it does in body. Knowing something in Mind is the starting point for all that manifests. Once something is "known," the union of thought and feeling brings a birth. The coming together of thought and feeling is the union of ADAM and EVE. This Bible story can be understood in many ways, but let's put it in the evolutionary perspective and see the two sons of ADAM and EVE as the two-sided nature of every human being. The story places us at the beginning of our human evolutionary journey. Since the duality of the GOD SEED is always expressing, there are, of course, two sons, CAIN and ABEL.

CAIN is described as a TILLER OF THE GROUND, so it is apparent that we must associate him with Substance. Because Substance has now reached its material stage, this means he is a body of atomic matter that is animated by a material viewpoint, or shall we say the UNDER side of his environment. His body can operate with only five senses so that he sees just a reflection of life and he believes that fulfillment comes from what he sees. The brain of CAIN receives electrical signals from his nervous system that conforms to his limited viewpoint and presents many sensations and desires. These are all on the material level and his limited view of Life and Substance permits only a brief and fleeting relationship with his brother ABEL.

The name ABEL means "transitory." ABEL also means "vapor" and since vapor is not fixed or tangible, ABEL is the mental body (field of energy) which is nebulous to the human senses. CAIN illustrates our human condition, very absorbed in the things of the material plane and whose mental activity is confined strictly to physical satisfaction. This tells us that as we began our evolution, ability to concentrate on anything, except what was visible, was weak and our attention span was childlike. Thinking about the cause of something, or perceiving the why and how of it, was impossible.

CAIN "feels" life but does not "know" it. He can only sense it; what it feels like, looks like, smells, tastes, and sounds like. The sense side of human nature is satisfied from what it sees on the outer level. CAIN has only a vague perception of mental capacities because his feelings are paramount. He typifies the lower human nature that does not yet appreciate the value of a relationship with his higher mental nature ABEL. He judges only by appearances.

ABEL represents our mental aspect that "knows" because he is the thinker. The Bible tells us that he is a KEEPER OF SHEEP and the word SHEEP is an important symbol used throughout Scripture as well as in other sacred literature. SHEEP represent living truths, or higher thoughts. Since ABEL is "transitory" and like "vapor," he represents a mental awareness, which at this early stage of evolution, is as misty and transitory as a cloud. This tells us that the higher mental field of energy (ABEL) is not yet fully active in the field of material substance. He is KILLED IN THE FIELD by his brother CAIN. The FIELD, or course, is the lower energy field of atomic matter. Nothing can live in consciousness unless there is an awareness of it.

Through this allegory we see that at the onset of evolution, primitive beings were not capable of much mental cognition. The undeveloped intellect did not have contact with higher vibrating frequencies of thought. This higher mental activity with its ideals of perfection was KILLED by the nagging desires of the senses. However, it is killed only in the manifest FIELD of matter, not in the higher dimension of Mind. Although it is true that the Christ ideal may be prominent in the human thought stream today, for all intents and purposes, its ability to impart Truth to an individual who is emotionally tied only to materiality is difficult. Such a person is ruled by the senses because the intellect has not yet developed sufficiently to allow higher perception.

So we see as evolution gets underway, that the first point of attention is on outer things, since the individual is subject to only the five senses and not to ideas. Since universal law requires that everyone contribute to the universe through the radiation of ideas, CAIN'S sensual contribution is not FAVORED by the LORD (law) of his being. What can a material being give to the universe? He can give only what he is in consciousness. If life is seen as only material, the only thing given to life and the law of being is that of the material level. Materialism does not promote evolution, but keeps the status quo, which is imperfect. The true idea of manifestation is perfection; it is this ideal of Life that is held in the Absolute level of Mind. Since nothing is progressed by CAIN'S offering, it is not FAVORED by the LORD.

This tells us that the mental nature, represented by ABEL, is of first importance to the universal scheme. It tells us that "what" we think about life is more important than "what we do." Why? Motive for any action is governed by awareness. Motive is more important than the act since it is the cause. What is "known" is the only real power, or we might say "consciousness" is the only reality. Actions are secondary to realization because they are only the result of present levels of thinking, so it is essential that one learn to think about the cause that underlies what appears. The moral of this story is that outer action means little if we are ruled and motivated by a material outlook that insists upon self-gratification or only selfish personal gain. The story of these two brothers reveals that outer things have no real value in themselves, but thinking (self-reflection) contributes to our evolutionary progress because it brings understanding, and therefore adds to the collective well-being.

This allegory also shows how the belief of death was introduced into the human experience. As CAIN, humanity is limited and confined to the idea of a physical body. This limited concept of body does not feel or comprehend its incorruptible, eternal body. This is because the archetype for that body resides outside of space-time. Only through ABEL, can the truth of everlasting life be known. ABEL is the aspect of self that can self-reflect and when contact with him is cut off, life is limited to physical, material conditions.

As one moves through evolution, eventually the questions are asked such as "Who am I, What am I, Why and How am I?" This is a sign that conscious awakening has begun. Of course, the CAIN side of human existence cannot ask these questions nor can it know anything about living forever. Material consciousness lives only for today with no concept of higher possibilities for what tomorrow can bring and looks only to maintain the status quo. CAIN is totally grounded without the help of his brother ABEL.

This materialistic view is not evil or disobedience, but simply ignorance of what eternal life is all about and that other realms exist outside of space-time. This ignorance causes fear and this is described by CAIN.

AND IT SHALL COME TO PASS THAT EVERYONE THAT FINDETH ME SHALL SLAY ME.

Fear of death is the result of being cut off from the nourishment of the higher mental capacity on the inner levels. CAIN feels a sense of separation from his natural wholeness which makes him insecure. He is all of us when this sense of separation from the truth brings about a desire to protect and defend. We become defensive because we fear losing whatever we consider our good. This defensiveness always brings problems, but at the same time the fear and insecurity that causes it, also acts as a catalyst to develop the will to survive, to express strength, courage, and steadfast perseverance. Many undesirable traits also develop. Such is the two-sided nature of being and since evolution moves upon a curve, both the positive and negative attitudes return to us and will bring either benefits or unpleasant consequences.

However, even suffering itself is a teacher and nothing is ever experienced that can't eventually be beneficial. How can humanity get free of the fear that causes defending, attacking, and suffering? Freedom comes through self-reflection and that happens as each experience teaches us to look for the invisible mental cause of problems. We can say that in spite of fear, or with its help, we gradually learn the truth about life. We should always be aware that both good and evil are in all things and the friction between these two helps promote our awakening to reality. Remember, we are functioning as the TREE OF KNOWLEDGE OF GOOD AND EVIL. We have chosen to see contrasts and this school of learning is a mixed bag of that duality.

SETH

Up to this point the Bible tells us that evolution has placed humanity in quite a predicament. Having lost contact with the higher mental body, no self-reflection is possible and life becomes difficult, but the great law always insists upon polarity. The law is that when the two separate, they can make another copy and once again become two. Our story presents a new brother for CAIN and his name is SETH, which means "substitute," "compensation." He is the new offspring of thought and feeling (ADAM and EVE) and he represents a lower mental body that knows only limited life and not the whole of life, as did ABEL. He will act as a substitute because he is an idea that the human being can accept. The true idea of eternal life is too big, too expansive, for this new race of beings to comprehend. SETH is the belief in temporary life that runs out of energy, depletes itself and experiences death. He is the belief that only so much life can be stored up in the body and when that is gone, death is the necessary result. He is the belief that Substance diminishes and deteriorates.

However, the Bible says that through SETH truth will eventually be known and eternal Life will be fully realized. This means that with the ability to self-reflect through a lower mental field of energy (body) even if the thinking process is limited, consciousness will ultimately expand until the higher the mental nature can once again be contacted at the abstract levels of Mind.

In the meantime, the wheels of evolution will grind slowly because human consciousness accepts the wholeness of Life and Substance only in small doses. Ignorance of the truth is understandable in our previous stages of evolution, but even today too few of the human races have yet accepted even the theory, if not fact, that the body does not have to deteriorate and experience death before it can live eternally. The fact is, we are in eternity now, and when we fully awaken, we will see that the material body can be spiritualized and death of the body is not a reality. Death is only a belief that has been caused by fear, as shown in this story. When self-realization occurs, the atoms of the body will reflect that awareness. This is fact, because what is in consciousness will manifest. It is the law of the TRIANGLE!

Chapter 6

FUSION THROUGH SACRIFICE

ENOCH

Next, we are given a little encouragement. Perhaps the writers of the Bible knew that if we could read the symbols thus far, we might be a bit dismayed about the struggle that lies ahead for the individualized soul. They give us an outline of how the great scheme of things will work itself out, by producing a genealogy. The meaning of each name in this listing can be found in the original Hebrew and they stand for prevailing states of consciousness as generation after generation passes through evolution. This genealogy discloses that many new states of awareness evolve as a consequence of experience on the material plane. In this progressive genealogy the name ENOCH appears. He is described as:

ONE WHO WALKED WITH GOD AND THEN HE WAS NOT, FOR GOD TOOK HIM.

Since we know that GOD acts as the triune Principle (law) and not as an entity that reaches down and takes people for reasons unknown, we must conclude that ENOCH was "taken" because certain conditions of being were met by the law of evolution. In other words, he was lifted up in consciousness to the extent that his realization about the eternal nature of the two ideas of Life and Substance so absorbed him that he could no longer stay bound to the material level. He translated his material concepts of Life and Substance into their true, unlimited state. He experienced the reality of eternal qualities and consequently transformed his material body into a spiritual, eternal body. His act of translation is a preview of what will happen to others in the Bible in later periods of evolution. Herein, we see how the creative Principle serves the soul. Since the physical body is the outer manifestation of beliefs of materiality, when those beliefs are translated into the higher language of spirituality, the body is also translated.

ENOCH may be an actual historical figure or he may be only allegorical. The essential thing to realize is that he illustrates how the law of vibrating thoughts acts in both the material and spiritual worlds. Through this account of body translation, we see that what is conceived in Mind, the body will achieve. As whole life is well established in Mind, whole life in the body is a natural consequence.

The genealogy and the story of ENOCH are placed here in the Bible to connect CAIN and SETH to the stages of development that follow at a much later time in evolution. It was inserted as a prophecy for humanity; to show that translation of the body is part of the Plan as evolution proceeds. Since we know that everything moves in continuous cycles, ENOCH could have been an initiate from a previous cycle of evolution. In that cycle, an earlier Race could have already passed from the material plane by transmuting the atoms of their bodies to the higher vibratory planes. It seems plausible that ENOCH is placed here in the scriptures as an example for those who will follow in this cycle of evolution and accomplish the same thing.

This should not seem impossible when we think about the power that is locked within an atom. When the atom was split, we saw that power as the atomic bomb! Since atoms are just the outer manifestation of creative energy that exists outside of space-time, it is not hard to believe that there is power within us that has yet to be tapped. However, we human beings have a long journey ahead of us to outgrow our belief in death. It is deeply embedded in the collective consciousness and is the last false belief to be overcome. It is comforting to know that even death can serve a good purpose by bringing continual new births which will promote the expansion of awareness. We are assured of this in the next story.

NOAH AND REINCARNATION

Because the belief in death had entered human consciousness when the killing of ABEL occurred, it had to be experienced by the human race. Why? Because thoughts held in Mind will be expressed! This law of consciousness rules supreme. After death, new bodies must be formed again and again until the eternal quality of Substance can be realized. The desire to express Life and Substance in a material way, or through body sensations, will cause repeated incarnations. This aspect of universal law and how it plays itself out in the great Scheme is illustrated in the story of NOAH and the ARK.

Again, let's keep the evolutionary perspective and go back in thought to the beginning of all manifestation. Picture the LIGHT from the higher levels descending to the lowest level of manifestation and then beginning its ascension as it gradually moves through matter. The descending lower planes of matter are so dense that little LIGHT got through in the early stages. First the LIGHT passed through the mineral kingdom, then the vegetable kingdom, then the animal kingdom. When each progressive, ascending action began, sense perception was brought more and more into play and free will was gradually established in material consciousness. By the time the LIGHT was experiencing through the animal level, instinct was working with the five senses, but self-conscious thought did not operate until the LIGHT was focused through the human kingdom. At that point, free will became the dominant aspect of being and conscious responsibility began. Through each kingdom, as another level of matter was experienced, awareness of the preceding kingdom was not lost, but incorporated into the next level. However, the limitations of that lower kingdom had to be eliminated on the newer level. At present, the responsibility of the human kingdom is to consciously eliminate any animal traits that keep Life and Substance bound to the material level. Once this is accomplished the spiritual level can be expressed through the human kingdom.

As we look at the story of NOAH we can imagine the process of evolution as atoms, then molecules, then cells all cooperating to make forms. Fossil records show this history which leads to the appearance of Homo sapiens. Old forms gave way to new ones. In the natural course of events the human kingdom came into being. This account does not necessarily suggest that humans were once animals, or vegetables, or minerals, but it does suggest that the individualized Christ consciousness, residing on the higher mental plane, had to penetrate its LIGHT (intelligence) through each of these material levels. The human body is made of the elements from all these kingdoms.

The physical body now adheres to the reflected pattern (TREE OF LIFE). It has a trunk, with a central spine that eventually stands erect so that it can act as a conductor for the energies that will propel it. Centered on the trunk is the head through which the LIGHT can be received, processed through a brain, and then dispersed through a dual nervous system. The trunk has two roots and two upper limbs, which are two triangles, one upright, with the other inverted. The human body is a living organism, but unlike others on the planet, it has conscious contact with other levels of Mind because it is a reflection of both the TRIANGLE Principle and its mirrored image. The appearance of the human vehicle was a significant point in evolution because once the LIGHT began expressing through the human kingdom it had come into its permanent home on the outer plane. The body is meant to be the perfect temple for the GOD SEED energy which is reflected through it. The lower kingdoms of mineral, plant, and animal are able to reflect only the qualities of GOD, but the human kingdom does this and more. It also reflects thought patterns which form conditions. The human being, although not conscious of it, is already acting as a co-creator with the Absolute GOD and has been given DOMINION through the power of MIND. Once the LIGHT entered the human stage of development, the GOD SEED could express its qualities and also be conscious of itself as "I AM" on the material plane. From this stage, that which had manifested would BECOME AS GODS (Gen.3:5)

As already revealed in the creation story, it was not until independent choice was developed that the LORD GOD (law) MADE COATS OF SKIN AND CLOTHED THEM (Gen 3:21). This certainly makes it clear that free choice and individual responsibility are prerequisites for attainment of the higher life. This is not understood by those tied to outer appearance and who want to perpetuate traditional ways of doing things. Free choice must be used so that the uniqueness of the "I AM" can be achieved. Each choice brings consequences through which truth is learned. In this way every individual can realize freedom from within.

THE FLOOD

The FLOOD of NOAH'S time can be seen as an actual inundation of water that swept away certain lower forms and preserved higher ones. It can also be seen as the time when certain desirable qualities, already being expressed in the lower, animal kingdom, were preserved. These qualities served as a bridge to extend the LIGHT into the next level of expression, the human kingdom. These desirable qualities were incorporated into the human kingdom and would be refined further as evolution progressed. The animals that went into the ARK, two by two, symbolize the dual attributes of the animal nature in the consciousness of the human being that have been transmuted into a higher state and are now valuable enough to be preserved. They will be "stored up" in the ARK which represents an energy field that is objective about the experience of the soul. It can be called the causal body, since it is a body of energy which is the cause and intention of the soul while it is embodied in the flesh of material Substance.

This causal body is the product of transmuted desire whose characteristic is love. It serves as a protective sheath (ARK) for the soul and has been built by thought and feeling. As lower, animal-like instincts are lifted into higher thoughtful expression, this purified energy is placed in safe keeping in the causal body energy field. Thus, with every thought, which is electrical energy, the soul builds a purified receptacle which preserves that which is in harmony with universal law.

The FLOOD also points out that evolution will progress through alternating cycles with each cycle reaching its peak at a new level (MT. ARAHAT). Every successive cycle will spiral higher than the proceeding one. New beginnings (leaving the ARK) will produce new worlds of experience and new embodiment for the soul, over and over again, as Mind energy is continually recycled. On each spiral of experience there will be some repetition of certain characteristics (DOVE returning when sent out by NOAH.). This return acts as a foundation for new insight and thus higher expression for the soul. The DOVE returned to NOAH twice; the second time bringing an olive branch, the symbol for love and peace which is the energy that restores and renews conditions after a changes take place. A RAVEN was sent out first but did not return. This bird feeds on dead things.

These events characterize the way we expand in consciousness. First there is destruction and the sacrifice of old things and conditions by the WATERS which represent the emotional nature as well as Substance. Then there is a period for cleaning up, or a cleansing process, and finally comes the experience of peace and love in the soul as new forms of Substance take shape. Some traits that are no longer advantageous for higher expression will be destroyed, while some will undergo transformation and be expanded for greater use. This activity is also symbolized by the animals, the family members, and people in the NOAH story, who are either preserved or destroyed by the WATERS of the FLOOD.

It is good to remember that Genesis has already told us the WATERS represent potential forces that are still in the unformed, unexpressed state. The WATERS are the GOD SEED'S unlimited Substance that is always active within us and bring us to new and higher performance. The FLOOD comes to each of us individually as we progress in this outer school for Mastership. These FLOODS might be called the tests and exams that must be taken to evaluate where we are in consciousness. A FLOOD experience is always an opportunity for realization about a particular situation or attitude. The insight gained from destructive forces brings new realization. Certain conditions that are valuable may be preserved and others may undergo transforming change. At the same time, anything or anyone that is no longer beneficial to us may be "washed away." Entirely new conditions may manifest after the FLOOD and new people more in tune with our new state of consciousness come into our life. A FLOOD experience will present a different self-image as the old one is "drowned." It is this new image of self that will bring newness into our life.

The protection of the ARK is important in this story. The ARK is a place of security within Mind and protects and promotes higher thought, and saves us from the buffeting, stormy conditions. The plan of evolution has provided a way of psychologically seeing us through storms until we feel safe enough to begin once again with our newly gained insight about ourselves.

A COVENANT IS MADE

AND I WILL ESTABLISH MY COVENANT WITH YOU, NEITHER SHALL ALL FLESH BE CUT OFF ANYMORE BY THE WATERS OF A FLOOD. NEITHER SHALL THERE BE ANYMORE A FLOOD TO DESTROY THE EARTH. AND GOD SAID; THIS IS THE TOKEN OF THE COVENANT WHICH I MAKE BETWEEN ME AND YOU, AND EVERY LIVING CREATURE THAT IS WITH YOU, FOR PERPETUAL GENERATIONS. I DO SET MY BOW IN THE CLOUD AND IT SHALL BE FOR A TOKEN OF A COVENANT BETWEEN ME AND THE EARTH. (Gen. 9:11)

Putting our story in a historical perspective, we see the development of the human Race has reached a new stage when conditions are ripe for a leap in consciousness. Body temples of the Christ are manifesting on Earth. The word COVENANT means "agreement." It indicates that a harmonious chord had been struck between the vibrating frequencies of the lower and higher planes, wherein the perfect pattern for humanity was being held in Mind. LIGHT had penetrated the density of the atomic body form to such an extent that some of its radiance was being reflected back into the inner planes.

This ability to self-reflect some of the GOD Intelligence, established the body form as the permanent temple for GOD expression. The criteria for the necessary energy exchange had been met, which permitted the next stage of evolution to begin. The outer structure now conformed adequately to the perfect pattern. This exchange of LIGHT (intelligence) formed a bridge of LIGHT and assured that the body temple would never be in danger of being cut off from the perfect image held in Mind. Here we should note that this preservation of the body is not the whim of a deity in "heaven," but is a cosmic and physical law. The body and Mind are one and what is held in Mind will manifest!

The Bible says that the body form at the time of the FLOOD was to be preserved for PERPETUAL GENERATIONS. This means that the manifested body idea is "agreed to" in Mind because it now conforms to the original CREATED idea of Life for MAN. It will be allowed to reproduce itself over and over again because the right conditions have been met according to established law. The reproduction will happen through reincarnation until the physical matter of the body is completely refined and perfected in the process. Reincarnation is the new beginning after the FLOOD; it is portrayed as the emergence of NOAH from the ARK.

The BOW IN THE CLOUD is the TOKEN OF A COVENANT. This BOW is the refracted LIGHT from the seven different wave frequencies, or currents, which appear as colors, and express as qualities, after having passed through triangular prisms in the process of self-reflection at each level. This spectrum of LIGHT appears as a BOW, which is SET IN THE COULD. This CLOUD is the veil of thought patterns that acts as a screen for these powerful forces of energy. This screen protects humanity from their full radiance which is of too high a voltage for the unrefined physical body and consciousness. Their high frequencies of vibration could destroy the bodies that have been built and must be PRESERVED until the fullness of Christ consciousness can be realized and fully manifested through them. Thus, the materially centered conditions of both mind and body are protected, but at the same time, LIGHT will constantly be available through these seven streams of energy. This is a BOW of refracted LIGHT that is within the CLOUD of human thought. It is cosmic energy which acts to promote evolution through a filtered process. A rainbow, which is refracted light as it passes through drops of moisture in the air after a rain, is a reminder of this esoteric truth on the physical plane.

The ARK is the resting place, the haven of protection. Esoterically, known as the causal body, this body is the field of energy occupied by the soul between incarnations. It is connected to the permanent atom of the individual soul that resides at the higher causal level. When consciousness is withdrawn from the body of flesh (death), we return to this state of being until desire to experience in material form once again draws us into physical embodiment. We can understand this causal body as one made of the original essence and it embodies the accumulation of all the [good] from many lifetimes. This body of [good] acts as an ARK to preserve that which will be useful to the universal scheme of things. Through multiple lives, eventually enough [good] is accumulated to translate the human form into the permanent temple. The word [good] is bracketed to indicate that we do not as yet really know what good is, except that it is a level of intelligence. The word is used in the Bible to indicate that certain conditions must prevail before the final leap in consciousness can be experienced.

Since the COVENANT means that harmonious contact has been made between the higher and lower planes, it assures that harmony in life is possible and can be maintained. The harmony comes through progressive leaps in consciousness and the Bible continues to use the symbol of the COVENANT throughout, to label such leaps. We are of course, still making periodic leaps in the way we see everything and it may seem to be taking a long time, to get to that permanent harmony. By human standards, it seems long, but by cosmic standards, all is proceeding according to universal law!

It seems everything has been provided for the scheme of evolution but our text tells us that there is one more detail yet to be established and we find it in a seemingly mysterious story.

Isn't it good to know about the Plan and that this Covenant (agreement) between the invisible realm and the visible was made? The physical body will only be temporary, but it will renew itself over and over again until the God Idea of a perfect body is realized in consciousness. Our evolution is assured. That means our ascension is also assured. How can this happen? It has to happen because God's perfect life and unlimited substance are invested and immersed into us. They will not be confined forever. Because of the activity of our thought and feeling, it is in constant movement from the lower to the higher and is gradually bursting out of the bounds of materiality.

Actually, we have more than one body. Since there are seven realms, with manifestation in each realm, we function in seven bodies in those seven even if we are not aware of that. Our lower three bodies are called the physical, emotional (astral), and lower mental. They function in the lower, outer manifest realms of the human planes. The three higher bodies are the higher mental, causal, and spiritual. The lower three bodies are connected to the higher three by the etheric body, which serves as a bridge between the lower and higher aspects of our body consciousness.

It is good to keep a crystal in a window that gets the sun.

When it catches the sun and reflects the seven rainbow colors, it can remind us of the seven realms in which we live, each a different and brilliant color vibration. That beautiful display was discovered by Isaac Newton long before our time. He found that passing light through a lens split that light into seven rays of light. Another law of our universe had been revealed! Every time we see a rainbow it can remind us of the Covenant that was established in those early days of our evolutionary development. The Bible next presents us with another law that will be necessary so that we may expand in consciousness. It is the Tower of Babel.

THE TOWER OF BABEL

Let's look more closely at the human who is going to be developed into a god. At this point in evolution the polar nature of the TRIANGLE has now manifested as both males and females on the outer level, with each having within themselves both male and female characteristics. Each individual operates with both thought and feeling. This dual way to "be" presents opposites when only senses are used. These opposites are the good experienced along with fear that good will be lost or taken away. "Me and mine," "can and cannot," "happy and unhappy," "sick and well," are indicative of the way opposites work through the senses. This dual perception brings feelings of loneliness, helplessness, and fear of being cut off from personal security. These insecure feelings might not seem beneficial for humanity, but they will serve to develop uniqueness. No two souls are to be exactly alike. The feeling of separation from good causes fear and human self-centeredness that must temporarily prevail in order to develop individuality. Acting from the need for self-protection causes selfishness and even though this seems contrary to the scheme of evolution, temporary selfishness is essential for the emergence of individualized egos. Through the ego's belief in separateness, each soul will express separately and uniquely. This is revealed in the quote:

LET US MAKE A NAME FOR OURSELVES-(Gen.11:4).

These words mark the time when the realization of being a separate person entered the consciousness of humans. Through the human kingdom, the LIGHT (intelligence) of the soul will experience being like every other person and at the same time being very different and separate from others. This is the realization of "I AM" on the manifest level. It is the natural progression from the animal sense of self. The animal does not "know" a personal identity because it acts with instinct through a group soul. MAN is conscious of self as an individual because he is the manifestation of an individual permanent atom.

Let it be understood that the use of the word MAN refers back to the MAN of the creation story. It is used in the generic sense to represent humanity and is not to be interpreted as sexist. Hopefully, it is clear to the reader that every member of the human race is both male and female, therefore even the term "it" is appropriate when used in conjunction with MAN.

In this allegory something called the TOWER OF BABEL is built. It is a symbol for the accumulation of material things as well as human accomplishments. These are not permanent and are really only tools used to gain full illumination about the self. However, people put great store in things and in personal achievement and until greater awareness comes, achievement is used to validate the personal self and make us important in the eyes of others. Immature spiritual understanding promotes the belief that achievement even makes us acceptable to GOD. Since things and human accomplishments do not bring lasting or total satisfaction, they fall short of fulfilling universal law. This is why the TOWER is destroyed in the allegory.

Spiritual law will not support and sustain anything that is built from the level of imperfection except the body temple image. It is PRESERVED FOR GENERATIONS. A consciousness of separation cannot manifest wholeness and permanence because in reality there is no separation, there is only the whole. The story says that BRICK is used for STONE. Showing the manmade material was substituted for the real thing. The word STONE in sacred writings represents Truth. In addition, SLIME was used for MORTAR, once again a substitute. By analyzing the purpose of MORTAR, we realize it has a binding quality, so it follows that it represents that which can bind all realms of experience together. The SLIME is the human level of love, or false idea of wholeness, which can't permanently hold together whatever is built. Human love is but a substitute for the Absolute all inclusive and unconditional love that gives Itself away to its MAN-i-festation. Human love is not sufficient to bind the Christ Self to the lower self. Realities (STONE) must be "known" and through wisdom, real love (MORTAR) becomes the permanent bond uniting the higher and lower selves.

AND THE LORD SAID, BEHOLD, THE PEOPLE IS ONE, AND THEY HAVE ALL ONE LANGUAGE, AND THIS THEY BEGIN TO DO; AND NOW NOTHING WILL BE RESTRAINED FROM THEM, WHICH THEY HAVE IMAGINED TO DO.

Everything is working just as it should be; in complete accord with the LORD (law), which carries out the scheme. Human beings have all the qualities of the original image within them (although latent) and they are all speaking and acting as a reflection of the one image. Nothing can prevent them from achieving anything they IMAGINE TO DO (image). But since they all act with accord (ALL HAVE ONE LANGUAGE) or manner of expressing, there is no variety to the expression of Life and Substance. Now the author of this story tells us how the law works to achieve diversity within the whole through individuality at the material level.

GO TO, LET US GO DOWN AND THERE CONFOUND THEIR LANGUAGE, THAT THEY MAY NOT UNDERSTAND ONE ANOTHER'S SPEECH.

This is the obvious result of building anything in the outer world in order to make a NAME FOR OURSELVES and yet it is absolutely necessary for the evolution of the ego's individuality. When our attention is centered in the outer personality and what we can achieve for ourselves, there is a sense of separation from others. As personal identity is developed and attention is focused upon the personality self, the feeling that no one understands our language is the result. How often we may say, "No one speaks my language," or "No one understands me." While in limited awareness, we seem to stand alone. Indeed, no two people are exactly alike; no two people can experience the exact same thing, but each contribute diversity to the whole It is the focus of attention upon the personality that keeps us in the sense of separation from our good and makes another's viewpoint seem like so much BABEL. The word BABEL in Hebrew means "chaos, confusion, nothingness." These words aptly describe the predicament of MAN as he becomes absorbed in the personal self.

The moral of the story for us in our present state of evolution, is that when we feel all alone and misunderstood, the way to correct that feeling is to turn our attention away from ourselves and our own petty desires, bringing ourselves into a sense of oneness with the whole. We must see ourselves as part of that whole and give something of ourselves away to others. This sharing permits union with the higher levels of Mind which nourish us and is a sure way out of loneliness.

The TOWER OF BABEL story also shows us how humanity is separated into different groups so it can develop different qualities of expression.

SO THE LORD SCATTERED THEM ABROAD FROM THENCE UPON THE FACE OF ALL THE EARTH; AND THEY LEFT OFF TO BUILD THE CITY.

The seeds (individual units of energy) are scattered to produce and multiply for the purpose of expanding the experience of Life and Substance throughout manifest level. With the dispersion, more than one CITY can be BUILT. A CITY is the consciousness of each individual "I AM." By the scattering of the seeds which can also be called souls, many CITIES can exist, each contributing variety and diversity. With dispersion, many different conditions and cultures lend color and quality to the whole. As souls experience by being distinct from one another, they weave a beautiful tapestry of wholeness (holiness). Through self-reflection, each one of us will retain our own unique abilities and characteristics.

IN THE BEGINNING all was sameness, now the possibility for unlimited diversification has been established. Everything is ready for the great scheme of evolution to unfold. The saga of going out and then coming in again and again now begins . . . .

[See Figure 19]

Figure #19

THE GREAT SCHEME THROUGH SEVEN LEVELS

Here we see the original unit of Absolute energy working out the great scheme of evolution through humanity. Since we are a perfect reflection of the GOD SEED planted in MIND, we have the plan within us, along with all we need to carry it out. Starting from the top of the circle, we see the Absolute Life and unformed Substance descending and then eventually turning on the circle to ascend through different levels of awareness and form. Finally, full realization of wholeness is achieved and human evolution is completed. Humanity has now on the ascending path.

It is uncertain how many cycles of evolution this process will take for each individual, but we can be certain that the whole scheme and the imprisoned power for that accomplishment is within each LIVING SOUL. Once an awakening happens in an individual, it seems that it is possible to advance at a faster because the vibratory frequency has increased.

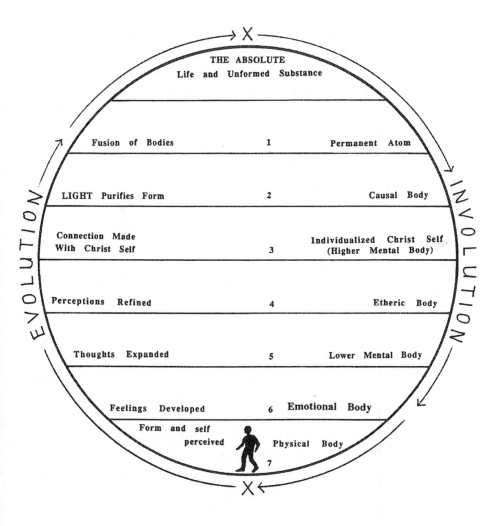

What a God! Every possible thing that would be needed to bring full realization to every unique individualized Christ has been provided. It is my hope that you now understand more about this totally encompassing, loving God, and that your trust in God is growing by leaps and bounds. There is nothing that can defeat us and there is nothing to fear. This story completes the explanation of the laws I found in the first few chapters of Genesis. They brought new insight into the rest of the Bible. The life of Jesus Christ took on a new dimension for me and filled my heart with thanksgiving and appreciation for His contribution to humanity. As we prepare to enter the New Testament, let's review a bit and see how the fields of energy that we are working with play a part in our final victory over death.

As this great adventure begins for humanity it is helpful to understand that there is a reciprocal law that embodies the entire process. We have seen how the "I AM" identity of the Cosmic Christ can produce many mirrored reflections of Itself. Each individualized Christ needs a material body in order to express on the outer level. In turn, the material body, including its lower mental, emotional, and etheric fields of energy (bodies) needs its Christ Self in order to exist. Let's recall again the TWO TREES, so that we may fully grasp the fullness of this law. After involution, the TREE OF LIFE stands as the perfect pattern for all the individual evolving Christs, but it is without tone, color, and the beauty that experience can give it. It is "potential" that awaits glorification through the many lifetimes that the TREE OF KNOWLEDGE OF GOOD AND EVIL will experience.

A good analogy might be that of a diamond in the rough which cannot reflect light because no facets have yet been cut into it. With the facets, it will reflect light in a brilliant way. Through each "facet" of experience, the personality releases the essence of the event; its pain, its joy, the triumph or defeat, the wisdom gained, the love shared, to the Christ Self (THE TREE OF LIFE). This return of energy "fires" or generates its energy into a rarified condition so that it gradually glows with radiance. We could compare this to a bellows pumping air into hot coals and seeing them glow in radiance and generate more heat. Through many exterior lifetimes the TREE assimilates the transmuted energy from the causal field "body" where it is stored from each lifetime. The TREE then reciprocates by giving back to the personality more radiant energy with life sustaining properties. Through this exchange of energy between the two, "the law of return" is practiced and they begin a fusion process that will eventually permanently unite them.

Now here is the exciting part! As the TREE OF LIFE becomes ever more brilliant, it literally becomes a tree of fiery energy. The energy eventually is so hot that it consumes the lower bodies (fields of energy). The personality, with all its fields of energy "bodies" is gradually consumed by the electrical energy of the Christ body. This is the refining process and it is described in the Bible many times through symbolism. Eventually, the lower vehicles are totally absorbed in the fire (higher energy vibration) of the TREE OF LIFE (the individualized Christ Self). When a fusion takes place between them the individual consciousness that has known itself as a person who is separate from wholeness no longer exists! That person has been "offered up" to his Christ Self through many rituals of sacrifice. This does not mean however, that the individual soul becomes extinct, but instead, that it has come into a different state of consciousness whose vibratory characteristics can only be speculation at this point in our evolution.

This ultimate sacrifice was depicted by Jesus and has been viewed by humanity as one of sorrow and pain. It has been misunderstood by mortal consciousness that cannot discern the meaning of its symbolism. This final ritual is really one of joy, as the personality self freely gives itself away to become one with the wholeness of the Christ Self, the TREE OF LIFE that stands eternally in the GARDEN of Mind. The two become one as the properties of both are fused together and the cosmic plan is fulfilled. This explains what Jesus meant when he said "I come not to destroy the law, but to fulfill the law." More will be discussed about this marvelous law of reciprocal action when we explore the true mission of Jesus Christ.

[See Figure 20]

Figure #20

RECIPROCAL ACTION

The reciprocal law works gradually to glorify every aspect of Being. As the lower bodies experience life on the outer plane, the essence of that life is returned to the Christ Self. This perfect pattern (TREE OF LIFE) continually feeds the personality and lower vehicle and energy fields with the outlines for perfection. It is "potential" waiting to be embellished with a uniqueness that can come only through individual material experience.

The Christ Self is "fired", or stimulated, by the essence it receives from the lower plane. The energy builds until this TREE OF LIFE is one of "burning" spiritual energy. When enough experience is gained, the Christ Self and lower self are in complete harmony with each other. In other words, the outer TREE OF LIFE conforms exactly to the perfect pattern of the inner TREE. This buildup of spiritual "heat" creates a circuitry which triggers a fusion between the outer and the inner bodies and they become one.

Just as a sense of separation tore them apart IN THE GARDEN of MIND, now the realization of oneness fuses them together. Evolution is a necessary exchange of energy, through self-reflection, that eventually will sustain a high level of performance for the Christ level of consciousness on all levels of MIND.

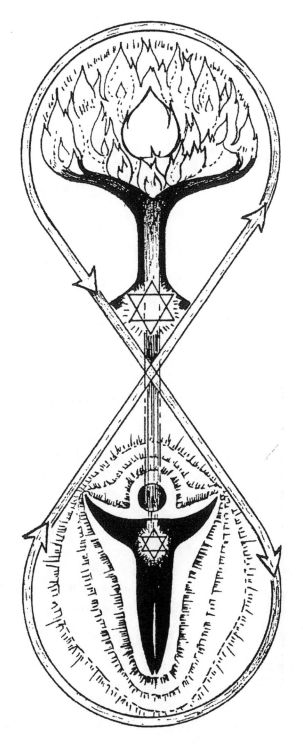

Chapter 7

WATCHING THE LAW
OF MIND WORK

Since you have succeeded in reading this far, you may be having second thoughts about what has been discussed in these pages. It is natural for us to think that we are foolish to elaborate upon the truths of the Bible. This kind of thinking is valid to some extent because any one person can't give another person the whole truth. Truth does not have an end because it is always pulling us one step beyond where we were before. The Bible is so complex, so filled with layers of meaning that attempts to untangle its web of truths may seem futile. Of course, no one interpretation of Truth can be the final one. What may be considered a revelation to one may not be to another and what has been written here is offered only as a possible implication of what the Truth ultimately is. These ideas should not be considered as an exact document of universal law. All that has been discussed is merely self-reflection and it is shared for the purpose of stimulating your own reflective power. Words alone can't make the Truth totally clear. After all is said and done, reading this book, or even writing it for that matter, might seem to be an exercise in futility because we don't seem to be much different than we were before we started. Ah, but this, of course, cannot be true!

It is well for us to remember that there is nothing more subtle than thought and feeling and what we have been thinking about and feeling within, is changing us. With only a limited amount of observation, it is clear that invisible thought and feelings are the only means by which anything or anyone is ever truly changed. In the meantime, all too often, the human self tries to rob us of new insight and keep us right where so-called "common sense" says we belong. Our personality self feels more comfortable with the old belief that we really are only mortals after all, and that the mysteries of life can't be known. It is true that our old identity needs a lot of convincing, since it does not recognize the invisible part of our being.

Since we are a product of the GOD SEED, like any other organism in the universe, we are developing in stages, and as we do, greater powers flow in and through us. Creation and evolution are not separate nor are they in conflict with each other. They are both an operation of Mind, impregnating invisible Substance with invisible Life ideas, which become visible matter that is animated by the fiery Life within it. Every idea is energy and has infinite possibilities for expression because the BEGINNING is always happening. This view of life should help us recognize the intrinsic value of everything that happens to us and through us.

The Bible presents a map for our evolution of consciousness and transformation of body through its many characters. In the Genesis story of Abraham, his life illustrates tests and realizations that trace the progression of human awareness through experience on both the inner and outer levels of Mind. His story and those of his ancestors in the nation of Israel are too lengthy to be included here. Let it suffice to say that they all metaphysically represent different stages of consciousness and development of the human race. To study them in this way is illuminating but that is for another book.

The message of this book is to fuse the science of today with the Genesis creation story. Truly, great wisdom teachers must have written the allegory of creation so that it could be understood at different levels of awareness. These teachers must have been from another cycle of evolution than our own, one that was more evolved. We have seen in the creation story that there are seven levels of consciousness which reproduce and expand their energy into many spheres and dimensions and that according to law, each sphere of consciousness will produce form. Therefore, it would be foolish to think that our humanity, in its present state of evolution, is the only expression of the GOD SEED.

Herein is the mystery of Jesus Christ of whom Christianity has designated as the Savior of the human race. Actually the name Jesus or Joshua, means Savior. Our story of creation would not be complete without an exploration of the science of Jesus Christ and His mission upon the planet earth.

We can begin that exploration by recalling the power in a seed. How amazing that a tiny flower seed can produce a thing of beauty! We cannot see the plan for that flower in its tiny seed with the physical eye, nor even with a microscope, but it is there. It will grow and flower if right conditions are met. First it establishes a root system that will feed and sustain its offspring. There are systematic stages of growth for the plant, each one acting as a building block for the one to follow. These stages of growth happen as a result of certain requirements being established in the environment in which it exists. When all is in harmony with the invisible plan for the seed, which exists outside of space-time, the visible physical plant produces a flower in all its glory. That flower also can produce more offspring and become many.

We have compared GOD to a seed and the creation story of Genesis has shown us that the plan for the offspring of that SEED develops by the same method. First it establishes a root system to feed and sustain its offspring and at each stage of development new building blocks appear. Each stage marks a period when new and different conditions develop as the creative process unfolds. They happen as a result of certain requirements being met until the plan within the GOD SEED produces Its offspring, "the only begotten son," which is the Cosmic Christ. This is the LIVING SOUL, or flower of the original SEED. It is helpful here to remember that all of this is the activity of two different frequencies of vibration. When certain frequencies are produced, their condition creates a new energy pattern. It is this new energy pattern that is the foundation for the next building block which will appear. Since the flower of the GOD SEED is made in Its IMAGE and LIKENESS, it contains the entire plan and can also reproduce. Thus, the Cosmic Christ produced many living souls known as mankind. Each member of mankind is also made in the image of the Christ and therefore contains the entire plan for "flowering" and the ability to reproduce.

With this understanding, we can see that every individual of the human race is a vibrating unit of energy which creates patterns that appear as events and conditions. It is clear that the human race must co-operate and harmonize with the invisible currents of energy that make up the plan for its development and eventual full "flowering." When certain requirements are met, or shall we say, when a certain vibrating frequency of energy is expressing, this allows a new building block to be established. History reveals that great teachers and leaders have appeared on the human scene to help bring understanding and expression to the new energy pattern that comes from the invisible and must be developed in the visible world. The Bible presents these way-showers to us as Abraham, Jacob, Isaac, Moses, and the Prophets. Each helped to interpret new energy patterns and to show the way to put them into practice in daily life. Each of them, acted as a building block for a particular stage of growth for humanity.

With this analogy in Mind, we can understand more clearly the appearance of Jesus Christ in the Middle East. The Hebrew people, with their unique belief in only one GOD instead of many gods, produced a frequency pattern that became a magnet for His incarnation. Hundreds of years before His appearance, their consciousness paved the way for new laws which were given to them by Moses. With the practice of those laws, they began a long journey toward the spiritualization of human consciousness. It was this concentration of belief in what could not be seen, and at the same time, belief that the invisible had contact with them, that formed an energy pattern receptive to the teachings of the Prophets. Down through the ages their longing for a Messiah (a Savior) created an energy pattern that made it possible for the anchoring upon the planet Earth, of the Cosmic Christ energy.

That energy could not be anchored on the human scene in its full tremendous power because the human race was not yet ready to accommodate that much electrical energy in consciousness or in body. Also, since the law established IN THE BEGINNING decrees that all energy must be assimilated and distributed through manifestation on the outer plane, there would have to be one who could act as a transformer to step down that power. In this way humanity could accept it through slowly developing stages of evolution.

Here, it could be helpful to recall an account of how electricity was brought into a rural area of Tennessee in the 1930's. The government built a power station and a transformer for the electric power, wired and placed a light bulb in the ceiling every home that was to receive the power. People waited and waited, but after many weeks the electric light bulb finally radiated with light. People ran out into the streets shouting, "The power is on, the light has come!"

The power station that was built for humanity is the Cosmic Christ and Jesus is the one who acted as a transformer, so that the tremendous voltage of that Christ could be stepped down for humanity. Thus His name, meaning "Savior" takes on greatness and His gift to the human race cannot, even today, be fully appreciated and understood. Without His willingness to act as the go-between for the Cosmic Christ energy and as the Way-shower to put this energy pattern into expression, the human race would not be able to advance to its full "flowering."

How is it possible that such a Being could do this for us? Surely, He must be an individual from another cycle of evolution, one who had progressed beyond the stage of human development and could understand what was required to set a higher vibratory pattern into motion. This was his mission, to anchor the new vibration of energy within the consciousness of humanity and penetrate it into atomic matter. This could only be done through sacrifice on the material plane. We have been seeking greater understanding of this sacrifice for two thousand years.

How true the saying, "When one door closes another one opens." A seeming miraculous event occurred when I was preparing to begin a new life without my husband. About a year before all of this, I had met a new friend at Unity Village in Kansas City, Missouri. I was attending school there, earning credits to become a Unity Licensed Teacher. She invited me to visit her in Ft. Worth, Texas, which I did some months later. After my visit, on the way to the airport for my flight home on a Sunday morning, we stopped to attend a large Unity Church in Dallas. The Minister, a well-known New Thought writer, was a fantastic speaker and the Church was very large and beautiful. "Oh, how I would love to teach here!" I told my friend. I was still married and there had been no talk a divorce at that time. It seemed an utterly foolish desire. There was nothing in my life that could make it possible.

Sometime later and seemingly sudden for us, my husband

and I reached a decision to divorce. We were both somewhat in a state of loss and shock, but we both felt our paths were going in two different directions and it was time to part. I had been a stay at home housewife after my marriage but there was something I knew how to do and that was working in a church. I knew how to teach metaphysics too, so I dared to believe that I could make a living doing what I loved. We decided I should write a letter to the Minister at the Dallas church. With my husband's encouragement I did write, telling him about myself and of my desire to teach in his church.

One morning very soon after this, I was in the kitchen doing the breakfast dishes when the phone rang. It was the Minister, calling from Dallas in response to my letter. He asked me if I could type and do office work and also if I had any tapes of the classes I was teaching. Making a tape had never been done, except the week before. One of my students had taped the class and given it to me. Was this more than just a coincidence? The Minister asked me to send it to him along with a picture of myself, which I did immediately. About a week later, he called again, "How soon can you get down here?" he asked. He told me that many Licensed Unity teachers had wanted to teach there but for some reason he felt I was the right person. We both felt it was more than just something called "luck" or "coincidence" and suspected that perhaps we had worked together in another lifetime as we progressed on our Spiritual journey.

The Church was rather grand with trees and a lake with white swans. This fine Minister interviewed me in his office and offered me the opportunity to work with him. He, as a memorizing speaker and teacher of Truth Principles and me, a lover of metaphysical insight into the Bible, seemed to fit together well to do the work we both loved so much. He was also a prolific writer and I had even taught one of his books to my class in Cincinnati. Little did I know then that I would one day be working with him! He hired me as a teacher, counselor, and director of the Healing Ministry and I later became his Assistant in doing all the work of a Minister. This wonderful man gave me opportunities and responsibilities beyond my dreams.

When I came to this wonderful, fulfilling work I was staying with my friend in Ft. Worth and he suggested I stay in his home which was closer to the Church. He and his wife would be out of town for two weeks. Another coincidence? It was fortunate for me and gave me the opportunity to look for an apartment nearby. Then I had a dream that showed me a lovely apartment building with a balcony overlooking a swimming pool. The next morning, as I was driving to the church, I saw a building that looked like the one in my dream. It had a for rent sign out front. Another coincidence? The Manager showed me the apartment but it was dark and not at all what I had envisioned. As I returned to my car disappointed, I suddenly realized there was another building right across the street that was an exact duplicate of the building I had just seen. I inquired at their office and they showed me the beautiful apartment of my dream. It was on the second floor with a balcony overlooking the swimming pool. Of course, I took the apartment.

Everything fell into place, new friends, an income to support myself, along with new skills to learn. I still had to gain some more credits in order to receive my Unity Teacher License and I was given two weeks off to finish my course and graduate at Unity Village in Missouri.

I had lessons about life to learn too. I was learning how to be independent and take care of myself. It strengthened me and also presented circumstances that gave me insight and wisdom which I needed in order to be helpful to those who would come to me to learn Truth Principles. It is essential to know them, but we also must practice them day by day as we go through life. How gracious is the law of life, which guides us step by step, when we trust that God's perfect life idea is showing us the way.

After almost three years in Dallas, the time came when it was apparent that I should continue my education to be Ordained and become Minister of my own Church. Reluctantly, but following my inner guidance, and with the helpful recommendation of my Minister, who had become my mentor and teacher as well as my Minister, I entered Unity Ministerial School. Gratitude for the wonderful opportunity and experience I had in the Dallas church still fills my heart and there are so many good memories. I am convinced that our inner Presence knows when and where we are supposed to be.

Sometimes we must even follow direction from that inner voice when it tells us to go somewhere that does not appeal to us. When I was in my second year of training at school a friend from Dallas asked me to accompany a group to Egypt. I had no desire to go to Egypt and had never been interested in that country, but there it was again, the inner voice. I had learned that I was never led astray when I followed it. "You must go" was the message. It seemed impossible! There were absolutely no excused absences from Ministerial School and this would be a two-week trip. Unless there was illness we had to fulfill our commitment to attend classes. No excuses!

My friend had traveled to Egypt several times and was in a program to financially help the Egyptian poor. She had arranged for our group to have a meeting with President Sadat while we were there. After making the decision to go, I hung pictures of the great pyramid, camels, and desert scenes, along with an airplane on the wall of my apartment so that I would see them every day. After a few weeks of affirming that I would make a trip to see these things, I went to the Director of the School to request permission to take the trip. I felt it would happen because I had imagined myself there every day! He did give me permission and asked me to share my experience with the class when I returned.

I felt I was supposed to go for some reason. Afterward I was sure. Here is what happened. When in the Kings Chamber in the Great Pyramid a friend and I started sounding "OM" over and over again while we stood leaning against the sarcophagus. The sound and vibration echoed throughout the Chamber and after a few minutes I experienced a tremendous heat and light in my head. It felt as though the top of my head was blown open. This was such an unusual feeling that it was somewhat of a frightening experience for me. I stopped sounding the "OM" at this point.

That night when I took off my shoes and socks I found that the nails of both of my big toes were black! It was as though they had been burned. Many months would pass before they grew out. It seems to me that this was evidence of either an injection of powerful energy or and awakening and release of energy within my body. Either would be the result of a vibratory change of energy in my body and consciousness. At that time I did not know as much about the power of vibration as I do now, but I was certain something significant had happened in that Chamber. Now I know that we are benefited by the vibratory patterns in sacred places on our planet, of which there are many. They are visited by thousands every year. I am sure many others are having similar experiences.

Recently, I read a book by Robert Hieronimus, Ph.D., who informs his readers about the King's Chamber in the Great Pyramid., "Tom Danely, a Sonics expert to NASA, tested the sonic resonance of the Great Pyramid. Researchers started out by lying down and humming in the Chamber's sarcophagus, which is cut from a single piece of granite. When speakers and amplifiers were activated in the Chamber they resonated and they found that the energy force was more powerful, the louder the tones were sounded. When Danely and his crew returned to their lab to analyze their recordings, they found that there was sound present in the Chamber even when they were not making any noise. The sounds were below the audible range, about half a vibration per second, or half a hertz. When they raised the tone enough to hear it, they discovered it was always in the key of F-sharp. According to the early Egyptian texts F-sharp is the harmonic vibration of the earth. Many Native American sacred flutes are tuned to F-sharp. Some speculate that sonic resonance was used in the pyramid to raise consciousness and for healing. Rosicrucians and Freemasons believe that the Great Pyramid was used to conduct rites of initiation.

My students through the years kept asking me to put my teaching in writing. Because of their encouragement, I began doing that shortly after Ordination while I was serving in my first Ministry in Roanoke, Virginia. In this next section an effort has been made to answer the most frequently asked questions received in classes, such as:

What is the Holy Spirit? Why did Jesus say, "No man cometh to the Father, except by me?"

How can the Immaculate Conception be true? Why the cross?

What was the true mission of Jesus Christ? Why is there another Creation Story in the New Testament?

Read on for these answers.

Chapter 8

FULL TRINITY ACTIVATED ON MATERIAL PLANE

JESUS CHRIST

The four Gospels of the New Testament tell of the life of Jesus Christ. Each is not only a historic view of His life but also presents symbolic steps in consciousness, if studied metaphysically. In the Book of John we are given an abbreviated version of the creation story of Genesis. John outlines the creative process with his opening statements:

IN THE BEGINNING WAS THE WORD, AND THE WORD WAS WITH GOD, AND THE WORD WAS GOD.

Christianity has taught that this passage refers to Jesus Christ as the WORD. There is no evidence of this if it is read as factual. In the second verse John reiterates his first statement just in case we did not get it the first time.

THE SAME WAS IN THE BEGINNING WITH GOD

Genesis says that IN THE BEGINNING two energies, one of Life and one of Substance, flow out of the original Source of energy. The combination of these three together created the TRIANGULAR foundation principle of all creation. This is the root system that will feed and sustain all that is produced from it. These currents of energy are released by the breath, or we could say, by the interaction between the radiation of Life and the magnetism of Substance. These different frequencies of energy being exchanged can be described as breathing because they are repetitive and cyclic. This breathing acted as an exchange of energy, which was not only WITH GOD but actually WAS GOD, just as John declares.

ALL THINGS WERE MADE BY HIM; AND WITHOUT HIM WAS NOT ANYTHING MADE

Who is HIM? Of whom is John speaking? He is explaining that what was WITH GOD is the action of GOD. It is the WORD of GOD which produces ALL THINGS. It is the Logos (Greek word for power). The Genesis writer told us this when he continually used the phrase, AND GOD SAID, to illustrate the establishment of each new level of creation. Through John then presents what was in these moving, sustaining currents of energy called the WORD.

IN HIM WAS LIFE; AND THE LIFE WAS THE LIGHT OF MEN. AND THE LIGHT SHINETH IN DARKNESS; AND THE DARKNESS COMPREHENDED IT NOT.

In this ever moving TRIANGLE, called the WORD, is LIFE itself and it is passed on to all creation. This LIFE was the LIGHT OF MEN but it was not recognized. The DARKNESS in which this LIFE was enclosed was not only dense matter but also the ignorance of human belief. Such a belief system was one that could not comprehend that the LIGHT (intelligent activity) was within mankind itself. Such ignorance believed there was a separation between GOD'S LIFE and human beings. Understanding of the true relationship between mankind and GOD was needed. Now the book of John tells us that something happens to bring new awareness to the human race with the following words:

THERE WAS A MAN SENT FROM GOD WHOSE NAME WAS JOHN. THE SAME CAME FOR A WITNESS, TO BEAR

WITNESS OF THE LIGHT, THAT ALL MEN THROUGH HIM MIGHT BELIEVE. HE WAS NOT THAT LIGHT, BUT WAS SENT TO BEAR WITNESS OF THAT LIGHT.

Who is this John? Christianity knows him as John the Babtist. He is a witness for the LIGHT. Is this the same LIGHT mentioned as the LIGHT OF MEN, which was not COMPREHENDED? In this scripture passage, "the light of men" is not capitalized, but the LIGHT, to which he bears witness, is capitalized. It is evident that "the light of men" at the stage of human development at that time, was different from the LIGHT to which John bears witness. He also makes it clear that even his own recognition of that LIGHT does not make him that LIGHT, but only a witness to that LIGHT.

THAT WAS THE TRUE LIGHT, WHICH LIGHTETH EVERY MAN THAT COMETH INTO THE WORLD.

In other words, the reader is being told that man's present understanding (limited intelligent awareness) is not the TRUE LIGHT.

HE WAS IN THE WORLD, AND WORLD WAS MADE BY HIM, AND THE WORLD KNEW IT NOT.

This LIGHT is indeed very powerful; powerful enough to make solar systems! Yet, it is not known by man. What a mystery! Can the LIGHT that is the TRUE LIGHT, to which John bears witness, help us clear up this mystery? We shall see. He goes on to speak of how this LIGHT CAME UNTO HIS OWN AND WAS NOT RECEIVED. He tells us that those who could receive him would be given the power to become "sons of God." This reminds us of the proclamation given to EVE by the SERPENT in Genesis 3:5 when it declares that they "will become as gods."

AND THE WORD BECAME FLESH, AND DWELT AMONG US (AND WE BEHELD HIS GLORY, GLORY AS OF THE

ONLY BEGOTTEN OF THE FATHER), FULL OF GRACE AND TRUTH.

The ONLY BEGOTTEN OF THE FATHER is the Cosmic Christ. Now one who is the perfect reflection of that LIGHT, one who is AS OF THE ONLY BEGOTTEN OF THE FATHER is presented by John. Note the words "AS OF." They tell us that this one is not the actual ONLY BEGOTTEN, but is one who is "AS" THE ONLY BEGOTTEN. In other words, this one is "like" Him and He is also "OF" Him, or made of the same "stuff" as the ONLY BEGOTTEN OF THE FATHER. He tells us that this one is the same AS Him, making Him the full expression of the WORD in the FLESH. This one is FULL OF GRACE AND TRUTH. John is introducing to his followers, one who perfectly and flawlessly will reflect the LIGHT which expresses as GRACE AND TRUTH. This one is the appearance of the whole activity of GOD LIFE contained in the original trinity of energy. He goes on to explain.

HE THAT COMETH AFTER ME IS BECOME BEFORE ME; FOR HE WAS BEFORE ME. FOR OF HIS FULLNESS WE ALL RECEIVED, AND GRACE FOR GRACE. FOR THE LAW WAS GIVEN THROUG MOSES; GRACE AND TRUTH CAME THROUGH JESUS CHRIST. NO MAN HATH SEEN GOD AT ANY TIME; THE ONLY BEGOTTEN SON, WHO IS IN THE BOSOM OF THE FATHER, HE HATH DECLARED HIM.

How does the Cosmic Christ DECLARE GOD? He will be DECLARED through one who was before John and who has received GRACE AND TRUTH. This one is Jesus Christ! Here is the first mention of Jesus by John. We see the realization of John, that a Being who evolved before him and having received the fullness of GOD, would now declare GOD LIFE as the LIGHT OF MEN. It will be DECLARED through Jesus Christ. Another word for DECLARED might be the word "demonstrate." Jesus would demonstrate through His actions as well as through His declarations the fulfillment of GOD in MAN. In addition, we shall see that another aspect of the mission of Jesus Christ, having received the full realization of His oneness with

God, will be to establish and activate in material consciousness the third aspect of the WORD, (the Logoic trinity).

The appearance of Jesus on the material plane as the full expression of GOD in MAN anchored the radiating action of the second aspect of the original trinity, which is the idea of perfect Life. Therefore, Jesus established in the material consciousness of mankind the vibratory pattern of the pure original Intelligent Idea of Life, which we know as the "Son" on the second aspect of the trinity. That Life idea is the radiating male aspect of the Absolute Power Source we know as GOD. The demonstration and sacrifice Jesus made on the earth plane set into motion the magnetic feminine aspect of that trinity. We know aspect as the Holy Spirit. All that manifests from the GOD SEED to MAN is the result of the three types of energy. They combine and their interplay results in action and reaction.

All three aspects must be activated through recognition, or shall we say observation, in Mind. The consciousness of Jesus Christ, who knew the Truth and law of His Being, acted to rearrange the atoms in the thought spheres of humanity. This change in thought patterns opened the way for the pure Intelligence of the Higher Mind to work through the consciousness of the individual soul. Figure #7 in this book presents a few ways in which to see GOD'S creative trinity and it may be helpful to review them in order to get a perspective about the mission of Jesus Christ.

Just as a plant, step by step, is supplied by the original plan for blossoming, so too, humanity receives from the invisible patterns of energy what it needs at each progressive step. Two thousand years ago, the appearance of Jesus Christ marked a significant change in the vibratory pattern of human consciousness. We shall see how His sacrifice on the cross marked a leap in consciousness for humanity. At the present time we are once again in the process of taking another leap in consciousness. Millions of people all over the world are learning and studying Truths that earlier would have seemed preposterous.

As you read this interpretation of the Bible, you may have sensed the importance of possessing a good measure of intellectual development and curiosity. One who is totally satisfied with what they presently know about life, GOD, and human behavior will not be interested in delving into the deeper waters of spiritual and scientific theory. That inquiry insists upon a great deal of self-reflection.

The Book of John makes it clear that one must have an illumined intellect to perceive these ideas. John represents those of us who have been "crying in the wilderness" of thought and feeling but now finally recognize that the full expression of GOD can be realized upon the earth plane by those that are able to receive it. It cannot be known all at once, but by degrees, through an awakening of the mental and emotional faculties and then by the demonstration in everyday life of the truth received. This is the promise as well as the challenge for the soul.

A PARABLE

When Jesus was asked what the Kingdom of Heaven was like, He responded by saying, "The Kingdom is like a grain of mustard seed, which indeed is the least of all seeds but when it is grown, it is the greatest among herbs." (Matt.23:31) The mustard seed actually produces a plant so large that it is called the mustard tree. He goes on to say, "The Kingdom of Heaven is like a leaven, which a woman took and hid in three measures of meal till the whole was leavened."

How profound is this statement when we understand the trinity. The leaven is the intelligent activity of GOD, the WORD, the LIGHT, which is hidden in "three measures of meal." These "three" represent the three aspects of the Trinity, which can be seen as Mind, Idea, Expression, and also as Father, Son, and Holy Spirit. All three must be anchored and activated on the material plane for the Kingdom of Heaven to be realized. The Holy Spirit can be understood as an energy force that builds new energy patterns as it overshadows physical atomic matter and human material consciousness, Jesus Christ appeared two thousand years ago to activate the entire trinity of GOD LIFE and He set about His mission with full awareness of how it was to be done and with complete dominion over all circumstances of the material world.

He would give humanity the gift of the Holy Spirit, which Jesus called the Comforter. It was to be activated in the material thought stream of the world. It must happen through a sacrifice on the material plane of the false belief about LIFE for the truth about LIFE. With this sacrifice, mankind would have the opportunity to reach its full potential, without it, the full flowering of the TREE OF KNOWLEDGE OF GOOD AND EVIL could not come about and the promise that "ye shall be as gods, knowing both good and evil" could not be fulfilled.

The plan that is within the "seed" (idea) of LIFE is not seen because it is outside of space-time and can only be fulfilled when a harmonious chord is struck between the visible and invisible vibrations of energy. Jesus would strike that harmonious chord so that all of humanity would have the opportunity of gaining its full potential. This is what He understood when He said, "No man cometh unto the Father, but by me" (John 14:6). He knew the result of His mission would make it possible for everyone to come into the consciousness of being "one with GOD." He said, "I and my Father are one." (John 10:30) and His mission was to arrange the vibratory pattern in such a way that it would allow all of humanity to know the same truth for themselves.

THE IMMACULATE CONCEPTION

How could the consciousness of the Cosmic Christ be anchored into the material world? Since GOD had established the law which decrees that whatever is held in Mind, will be expressed, it would have to happen through the receptive state of consciousness of someone in the material world. The Christ could not enter the material world except through a receptacle of consciousness, since the law requires that all things first exist in Mind and then in manifest form. Only a soul that had developed a consciousness of complete surrender to the spiritual, invisible activity of GOD and a purity of the GOD thought could be such a receptacle. That one was Mary, the mother of Jesus.

The Christ would have to appear on the physical scene, as a physical being, in order to radiate the Christ energy upon the earth plane. Therefore, there would have to be a magnet of consciousness that would be able to draw that Christ energy pattern into the material world. Mary acted as that magnet and the body of Jesus would act as the vehicle to radiate that energy into the atomic matter of the world. Here we see the co-operating two vibratory patterns, radiation and magnetism, at work in human evolution.

The Bible tells us that preparation of a consciousness that could receive the Christ had been going on for hundreds of years through the Hebrew people. A group known as the Essenes, were Hebrews who had chosen to separate themselves from others in order to form a community that would not engage in merchandizing, but in teaching, worshiping, and healing. Material gain was not their goal, only a building of a consciousness of GOD.

Among these, many scholars of the Bible believe, lived Mary. Women of the Essenes, had for generations, been taught from childhood to aspire to be the mother of the Prophet that would be the Savior, or Messiah, of His people. This group consciousness with its intensive instruction, taught an attitude of purity and surrender to GOD that eventually formed a vibratory pattern that could receive the LIGHT. This LIGHT was the "seed" idea of the Cosmic Christ.

Since we know that everything takes place in Mind, or outside of space-time, it is not difficult to believe that a seed of any kind is first an idea in Mind before it becomes a physical manifestation. This is the law! While living in this vibratory pattern of energy that the Essenes provided, and dedicating herself to serving GOD, the Christ idea took root in the mind and heart of Mary where it gestated and made a copy of itself in her womb, (the physical world) to eventually manifest as a physical expression of the Christ. This is the Immaculate Conception. This virgin birth took place through the purity of Mary's consciousness.

Surely, Mary must have been the most advanced soul upon the planet at that time and probably came into incarnation for this specific purpose. She would magnetize the new energy pattern so that the plan of evolution could enter into its next stage. Both Jesus and Mary were most likely souls that had already evolved in another cycle of evolution on this planet. Their understanding was beyond the human level of consciousness. They were worthy enough to take on such an assignment.

We know that there are higher levels of consciousness and it is possible that the Cosmic Christ is already completely established on higher levels. Surely this must be so on the Solar level of Mind, which is the highest plane that works through physical matter. Since the law provides expression of Mind on every level of creation, it follows that there are Solar Beings as well as human beings. Jesus and Mary could be from that plane of expression. The process of evolution is continually going on and there are others who have gone before us and others that will follow us. There is no end to GOD'S creation because it has been established in Mind and ideas held in Mind are infinite.

Scripture shows that Mary became a force field of magnetic substance able to receive the seed (LIFE) of GOD, which is the LIGHT. This LIGHT, or heat, radiates from the Solar level of Mind and its radiation stimulates the rotation properties of atoms. Jesus as a Solar Being, was a power station releasing that LIGHT to mankind. He dispersed this accelerated rotation as a force. This powerful force of energy entered into the atomic matter thought sphere. Since thoughts are electrical energy, His spoken words, the expression of His conscious oneness with GOD, moved and rearranged the atoms of the material plane. He told His followers that His words were Spirit and Life but they had little understanding of their significance to human evolution. The frequency of vibrations on the Solar plane could be described as "love" or "perfect harmony."

We can be inspired by the story of Jesus in the Bible but the birth of Christ must be more to us than an intellectual discovery. The birth as an inner experience of love being "given" to us and through us is the result of the receptive consciousness that is able to recognize the presence of GOD within. This inner birth makes it possible for us to understand the words of Jesus when He said:

GOD SO LOVED THE WORLD, THAT HE GAVE HIS ONLY BEGOTTON SON; THAT WHOSOEVER BELIEVETH IN HIM, SHOULD NOT PERISH, BUT HAVE EVERLASTING LIFE.

Jesus is not telling us that we must believe in Him, as the personality that appeared two thousand years ago, but that we must believe in the ONLY BEGOTTEN SON, whom He called His Father. When we can discern that this LIFE and LIGHT is continually sacrificing Itself to produce humanity and sustain it as it awakens to full completion, then there will be no such thing as death, but only everlasting life.

This same LOVE was acted out by Jesus when He gave Himself to the cross. That was a ritual performed by Jesus because He understood how the Cosmic forces work as a law of physics, as well as a law of consciousness. He knew that both are the activity and interplay of energy forces. With His sacrifice on Golgotha, in Hebrew means "place of the skull." The mental vibrational activity of Jesus established a new phase of evolution for this particular Earth cycle was set into motion.

Let's remember the maxim, "as above, so below." We must add that for EARTH to receive HEAVEN, "as below, so above," the two must harmonize and be perfectly balanced. The analogy of music might serve to clarify this point. If someone was singing a song and you wanted to join in, you would have to know the melody or be able to sing the harmony in order to blend your two voices together in a harmonious way. Otherwise, it would not be a good experience. Through the same law of vibratory action in music Jesus harmonized the "above" vibrations with the "below" vibrations. This set into motion the plan for the blending of the two.

Through Jesus Christ, with His unconditional self-giving love, the doors to the next level of experience were thrown open for all those who want to enter. It is described in the Bible as the "renting of the veil in the temple." This is the veil of illusion that keeps us out of the "Holy of Holies" in the temple that is not only the flesh body but also the error consciousness of unbelief. This illusion insists that death is the way to a place called Heaven. Jesus corrected this error in belief by demonstrating that Mind has DOMINION over matter when He resurrected His body. Few, as yet, have fully understood His demonstration of eternal life.

His words in John 12:49-50 make His mission clear: "For I have not spoken of myself, but the Father which sent me, He gave me a commandment; what I should say and what I should speak and I know His commandment is life everlasting."

Remembering this commandment, we, like Jesus, through the application of the laws of life that He brought and demonstrated, can now enter through the cross. Entering by the way of the cross has not yet been fully understood by the average Christian. Of course, we do not enter by literally hanging upon a wooden cross that stands on a barren hill, but through the Cosmic Cross. This Cosmic Cross is our "highway to Heaven," so to speak. Jesus extended the Cosmic Cross into the material level, putting it within the reach of all human beings, so that we may all use it regardless of race, religion, or creed. Everyone can come into His "Kingdom" of consciousness because of His sacrifice, which caused an acceleration and penetration of the GOD SEED energy into the material plane.

THE COSMIC CROSS

Surely, Jesus chose the Cross for His sacrifice to symbolize the Cosmic Cross and its active participation in our lives. In this symbol is the secret of how Life and Substance moves from one level of expression to another in our solar system. At first they are restrained, but gradually, in spite of that restraint, they expand their former limits until final expansion is reached. Through Jesus, the symbol of the cross has been anchored in the consciousness of the human race. With it has come an awareness that sacrifice is required in order to move from one condition to another. However, all the ramifications of this sacrifice are difficult to grasp and have not been thoroughly understood even though two thousand years have passed. Remember, GOD's time is not our time and the wheels of evolution turn slowly because we can only receive higher accelerations of energy a little bit at a time.

To fathom the significance of the cross, let's again go back to the creation story with its hidden Truths.

Through our imagination we can enter the Cosmic level of Mind and once again see the original LIGHT, which is a vibrating unit of energy, dividing Itself and spreading in two directions.

- The original point of LIGHT has two aspects, or "waves" of vibrating motion and these establish the underlying principle for all creation.
- This Principle is self-reflective and its mirrored inverted images spread in four directions.
- These four directions, or "waves" of energy, act as the four elements of our solar system.
- This dispersing of energy in four directions can be seen as the Cosmic Cross, a fourfold outpouring of radiating fire energy, or LIGHT.

[See Figure 21]

Illustration #21

SACRIFICE OF THE COSMIC CHRIST UPON THE FOUR ELEMENTS

Placing the GOD SEED as the central "dot" in the Mind (BEGINNING) and recognizing that it has four "waves" of LIGHT within itself, imagine a simultaneous movement of this LIGHT, in four directions.

It moves both horizontally and vertically. As the LIGHT continues to extend itself in four directions, it is also moving in a circle. Thus, a complete cycle of movement returns it to the starting point. This causes two spheres of activity for this active intelligence. These spheres interpenetrate and also reflect upon each other. The original remains whole at the starting point while it disperses its essence in four directions through its own mirrored reflection, THE ONLY BEGOTTON SON OF THE FATHER. This image or reflection of the original LIGHT is stretched out upon the Cosmic plane as a cross. This is the sacrificial act of crucifixion on the Cosmic level of Mind, through the Son. This ONLY BEGOTTEN is continually sacrificed upon the cross of four elements: fire, water, air, earth in order to sustain creation.

Manifestation takes place as LIGHT (energy) moves through the four elements, which are essential for building forms, so that the GOD SEED can experience its Life and Substance on extended levels of Mind. The Son is given to and consumed by the four elements, just as a seed is consumed by the plant. This is how the LIGHT comes into the world of manifest forms. The four elements absorb the LIGHT and therefore we see how GOD SO LOVED THE WORLD THAT HE GAVE HIS ONLY BEGOTTEN SON (John 3:16). The world of form could not exist without this Self-giving process. Human beings could not exist if this LIGHT was not within them. As Genesis illustrates, the GOD LIGHT radiance is reflected through the Son and the Son in turn, reflects this LIGHT so that it can be radiated throughout the lower manifest kingdoms. The purpose of this radiation is to spiritualize the condition of dense material substance.

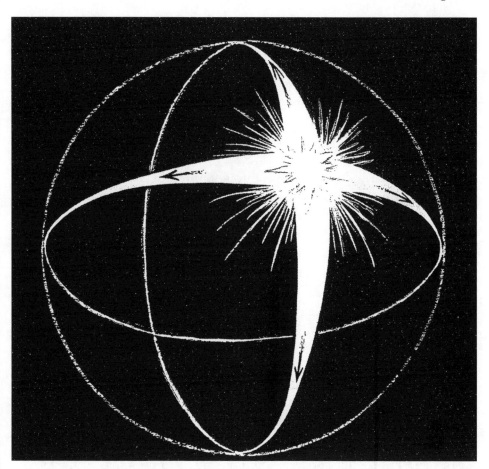

Again, insight comes when we read the words that describe the role of the Cosmic Christ: WITHOUT HIM WAS NOT ANYTHING MADE THAT WAS MADE (John 1:3). The New Testament brings us the story of how this law was understood and perfectly expressed through Jesus. As the Christ Intelligence continues the practice of Self-reflection, with each reflective state through successive levels of Mind, the radiant energy of the Absolute is somewhat diminished to accommodate manifest forms. This results in a diminished consciousness of its purpose. The meaning of this sacrifice becomes obscure by the time it reaches the manifest level of the world.

This sacrificial giving of the Cosmic Christ is continually going on. We can observe this ritual through nature as the seasonal changes when each one of the four elements takes its turn to express. The Equinoxes and Solstices denote the ever moving cycles and release of Life and Substance through the elements. Cosmic activity and its relationship to the human kingdom must be understood. Why? Because the way to a higher level of experience is not through a particular religion or creed, but through conscious inner sacrifice of error belief about Life and Substance and how it works through universal laws.

Hopefully, seeing the activity of GOD in a scientific way, rather than through traditional religious dogma, can remove barriers of belief that separates us from realization of our Oneness with GOD and from each other as human beings.

The universal laws were known by Jesus and He reaped the benefits. Not only does He benefit, but so do all of us. At this very moment and every moment, His awareness is constantly releasing the next level of vibratory wave patterns that will bring us fully into our consciousness of oneness with GOD. Knowledge of the universal law of sacrifice and the state of Christhood for the individual was not possible for the masses before Jesus symbolically re-enacted the Cosmic sacrifice upon a cross that stood on the material plane. At that time there was a fusion of energies between the higher and lower planes.

We could say that Jesus heard the song that GOD sings and was able through His thought patterns and His actions to not only harmonize with it, but hit the exact sound pitch of the universal song. The Bible illustrates the merging of these electrical forces as the thunder and lightning that occurred at the Crucifixion. Since the characteristic of the GOD song is self-sacrifice outside of space-time on the invisible level, the same characteristic of sacrifice of self was needed on the visible level in order to bring the two together. Here is the union, or mystical marriage that is the intention, or goal, of Spiritual LIGHT. Here is the merger between HEAVEN AND EARTH that was explained to us in the scripture of Genesis.

Jesus said, "***He that believeth on me, the works that I do, he shall to also, and greater works than these shall he do, because I go unto my Father.***" (John 14:12) This was His promise for all those that wanted to follow Him in the work of awakening to the truth about

Life and Substance. The commandment of His Father was eternal life and through Him was demonstrated Mind over matter.

Once the law is understood, it reveals so much about Jesus. How good it is to know that the same laws He used, are also available to us. We are awakening at a more rapid pace today than ever before. We can expect to know more than ever before. Scientific evidence says that the planet Earth is rotating faster than ever before. This means the vibratory frequency is being stepped up. Time and events are moving faster. The entire Cosmos of our particular system is evolving and changing at a more rapid pace. This can have an adverse effect on some, causing sleepless nights, more agitation, nervousness and fear and even mental illness. Others benefit, because they are also vibrating at a higher frequency and feel in harmony with rapid changes. The more willing we are to let go of the old ideas and move on to the new ones, the easier coming events will be for us.

Our planet is evolving, just as we are evolving. In fact, the entire Solar System is also evolving and each part of it, including us, must get into position to benefit this evolutionary movement. We hear about new and unusual alignments of stars and planets and some people are predicting a colossal change in 2012. No one can really accurately predict these kinds of things, but it is interesting to think about.

All this presents a good reason for me to share another dream with you. This is another one in which I had my second encounter with the great Being of my first prophetic dream. It happened while I was still working in the Dallas Church.

Again, I walked into a room with an opening about seven feet high and twelve feet wide. Standing to the right, was this same individual I had seen in my prophetic dream. He was dressed the same as before and as his loving eyes met mine, again I knew he was there to help me. What I saw in the opening was rather astounding and frightening. Because he was there, I knew it must have a profound meaning. Before me was the vastness of space. There were two planets that looked exactly the same but the one closest to me was larger than the one in the distance. They both looked like the planet Earth and the larger one was rapidly moving through space toward the distant planet. Alarmed, I said, "It looks like our planet is going to crash into the other planet that looks just like the earth!"

He replied, "There is no need for concern, the Earth will proceed on its way and those who are not ready to go on with the Earth will be removed and placed on the other planet."

Suddenly, I was certain that I would continue with our planet Earth, but I was still alarmed. "Oh, how terrible for those put on the other planet, what a shocking, awful experience!" were the words that came tumbling out.

Again, in his gentle voice, he said, "Not at all, they will go to sleep as usual and awaken to a world that is just the same as they have known before. They won't know what happened or think anything is different." The dream ended.

Years later, after I was Ordained and serving in my first Ministry in Virginia, friends took me to a mountaintop Meditation Center. We entered a peaceful lobby area with paintings displayed on the walls. I immediately approached one that portrayed a familiar scene. It was the exact replica of my dream of the planets! Although years had passed, I remembered well the same colors and the movement of the Planet Earth depicted by swirling lines in the painting. The painting illustrated a possible collision of the two planets. I was overwhelmed at the similarity with my unforgettable dream.

The Director of the Center approached and I told him I had a dream just like the painting and asked him what he thought the painting meant. He looked deep into my eyes, not speaking for a moment, and then said, "You know what it means," turned abruptly and walked away. I was left with my own interpretation.

When I had the dream, nothing about Planet Earth changes, Guides, and Ascended Masters were known to me. Over the years through much investigation, I have become familiar with the teaching of many Ancient Religions, Philosophies, Secret Mystery Teachings, and Beings of other dimensions of MIND that help the evolution of humanity. The Planet dream was one that I had to figure out gradually as time passed. Now I realize that our entire Solar System is evolving, moving, changing, and undergoing a change of vibratory frequency. Perhaps my dream indicates that in my lifetime, our Planet will make a leap into a higher thought stream (orbit), just as we in our personal lives, make such leaps into new ways to understand things that are happening in our world.

The same laws are always working on every level and in every dimension, all the way from the Absolute Source to below the atomic level. If we can break out of the limitations of our own individual experience and imagine ourselves as a part of the greater and boundless whole, as a Solar system and a Cosmos, we can accept signs of change more easily.

You are free to decipher the meaning of this dream. However, I will add that many philosophies and also the Bible predict that humanity will be separated into three parts as we proceed through evolution with one third left behind to follow later. Since Genesis tells us that nothing is forced upon us, it is clear that we will be wherever we choose as a result of the thoughts we hold in our mind.

Jesus speaks of great changes and the separating process in Mathew 24 and 25. He refers to the coming of the "Son or man." Of course, this "Son" is the LIGHT, or Sun in man; "*the Light that ligtheth every man that cometh into the world.*" This realization that we are LIGHT will not come to everyone at the same time, but according to the individual's chosen progression of consciousness. We are all programmed for enlightenment, but the pace of pursuing it is according to the free will of the individual.

Remember, dreams speak to us through symbols. The two Earth Planets in my dream represent different states of consciousness. Therefore, every individual will be in the environment they choose consciously and can imagine for themselves. Whatever mind images becomes the experience because consciousness is the only reality.

Actually, what we "see" as our place in the scheme of things is made of tiny pixels of light gathered together to appear in a form. We have the free will to create what we "know" and "believe." Will there be great disasters on our planet at a certain time? No one knows this for certain but we do know that a great change in consciousness is due for this planet. It is well to always be aware that our individual awareness of the truth about Life and Substance is important and contributes to evolution. What do you imagine for yourself and our planet? Why not imagine peace, harmony, and co-operation among all of mankind? How about seeing yourself possessing wisdom and acting always in love? What we concentrate upon in MIND will manifest!

Chapter 9

MINISTRY AND MISSION
OF JESUS CHRIST

The teaching that Jesus brought to humanity was one that moved atoms and built new archetypes in the Minds of civilization. His sayings were shocking to most of those who heard Him and little understood. Probably, it was the vibratory waves that radiated from Him that drew followers even more than the words they heard Him speak. Let's not forget that energy is vibrating at different rhythms in the atomic plane of the material world, according to individual consciousness.

Also, let's remember that every atom has within it the power to discriminate. That is, within the atom itself is the ability to select the electrons to which it will attach itself. Within it also is the power to regenerate and to reproduce. Quantum physics shows us that leaps from one level to another takes place and the teachings of Jesus help bring these kinds of leaps in our consciousness. This happens because everything is energy.

Jesus was able to rearrange atoms and to use the vibrational power of His spoken words to perform so-called miracles. Of course, they were not miracles, but the natural outworking of the law as it expressed through His consciousness. Actually, there are no miracles, since the law of consciousness is always at work. That is why, like Jesus, we must learn how consciousness operates and how to get in harmony with the vibrational song that GOD is always singing.

Every event in the life of Jesus is a symbolic illustration of different states of consciousness and how leaps from old beliefs to new ones can take place. The ministry of Jesus naturally brought about healings because of His vibratory radiation and because He was always aware of the wholeness of individuals, rather than what was appearing. He tells the people.

John 8:23: "*Ye are from beneath, I am from above; ye are of this world. I am not of the world.*"

These words take on great significance when we realize that a material consciousness sees only from beneath, sees only partially, and not the whole. The higher realm of awareness in which Jesus functioned always saw the whole, perfect pattern and that brought forth any healing that was necessary.

As wonderful as the healings were, however, they were not the mission of Jesus Christ. He continually identifies Himself to His followers in order to make His mission clear. The following are a few examples:

John 8: 58—"*Before Abraham was, I am.*"
John 10:30—"*I and my Father are one.*"
John 8:12—"*I am the light of the world; he that followeth me shall not walk in darkness, but shall have the light.*"

This identifies Him as a Being that existed before the Ancients of the Hebrew people, perhaps from another cycle of evolution. He is one who has an awareness of total oneness with the invisible Source of power. He radiates that LIGHT for others to follow. He said/

John 5:4—"*Ye are the light of the world.*"
John 10:34—"*Is it not written in your law, ye are gods?*"
Matt. 5:48—"*Be ye perfect even as your Father in Heaven is already perfect.*"

Without awareness of our oneness with GOD, such an admonition seems impossible to attain. However, with awareness that we are also that LIGHT with the capacity to reflect the perfect nature of that Source of power, we can see there is a possibility of perfection. Jesus explains that He is a mirror image of the Father.

John14:6—"*He that has seen me, has seen the Father*

He also explains that no one has ever seen the invisible Father, but that He is the visible image of that Father. How does the Father express? Through self-reflected images! Genesis has shown us this universal law. When asked about the Kingdom of God, He replied in the way:

Luke 17:20-21—"*The kingdom of God cometh not with observation; neither shall they say, Lo here! Or Lo there! For behold, the Kingdom of God in with you.*"

There is no need to look for the Kingdom as a place, it cannot be observed by the physical eye because it is hidden within us! There is a Kingdom of vibrating ideas in Mind and it is in these vibrations that we live, move, and have our being. It is a state of MIND. He tells His followers to stop looking outside of themselves and go within to find the treasure they seek. He knows, however, that the full realization of this will come in stages and it is explained in an example.

Mark 4:26-8—"*So is the Kingdom of God, as if a man should cast seed into the ground; and should sleep and rise night and day, and the seed should spring and grow up, he knows not how. For the earth bringeth forth fruit of herself, first the blade, then the ear, after that the full corn in the ear.*"

We have seen how the law works to bring the invisible pattern which is outside of space-time into visibility. We go about our business day by day and the seed, the idea of perfection within us, which is the Kingdom, knows how to step by step produce the finished product. Each stage of development is a building block for the next one to appear. We know not exactly how this occurs but nevertheless it happens in stages of development. Jesus also persistently tells us how to lift our belief about our identity to a higher perspective.

John 8:32—"*Continue in my word . . . . and ye shall know the Truth and the Truth will set you free.*"

Only the truth about Life and Substance can set us free from the bondage to material identity. The truth will reveal our spiritual identity and we will be free from the physical limitation of atomic, material substance and its physical laws. He does not say that He will set us free, but the Truth will accomplish this. His mission is to open the way for us to follow Him.

He outlines this mission again and again in His ministry:

John 14:12—"*He that believeth on me, the works that I do shall he do also; and greater works than these shall he do; because I go unto the Father.*"

Here He links Himself with His followers; they shall also do great works and that will be possible because of His mission. He will go to the Father.

John 14:6-"I *am the way, the Truth, and the life, no man cometh unto the Father but by me.*"

That statement is often quoted and has caused a great deal of confusion among Christians when they see the validity of other religions. Jesus never speaks from His personal self; He always speaks from His real identity as a Christ. His mission is to open the way for all humanity, of all religions, races, and creeds, to go to the next level of consciousness. Everyone, who makes this leap into the higher frequency of vibrating energy, will accomplish that only because of His sacrifice on the cross, which changed the prevailing vibratory pattern of the planet.

It is not necessary for an individual to believe in the person called Jesus, or even to know His teaching, for there is more than one path to the next level, but it was Jesus who broke through the "sound barrier" which is the lower vibration of energy patterns. His action makes the next step in human evolution possible for everyone. He explains an important part of His mission to His disciples.

John 16:7—" *It is expedient for you that I go away, for if I go not away, the Comforter will not come unto you, but if I depart, I will send him unto you.*"

John 14: "*The Comforter, which is the Holy Ghost, whom the Father will send in my name, he shall teach you all things, and bring all things to your remembrance whatsoever I have said unto you.*"

As already mentioned, this definite and important part of the mission of Jesus Christ should not be overlooked. The Holy Ghost is the whole activity of GOD and is the third aspect of the original triune creative principle. It was described as Spirit, or "wind" in Genesis. This current of energy will now become fully accessible when adequate self-reflection occurs in an individual. That energy pattern can provide what is needed as instruction, inspiration, and wisdom. This protective, comforting and higher intelligence will be activated as a result of the harmonious chords between the higher and lower planes being struck by the self-giving of Jesus Christ.

Scripture says that the veil in the Temple was rent when Jesus was crucified. We can think of this temple as our "house" of consciousness that has had a veil of ignorant beliefs that separated us from the full activity of GOD working in our lives. This was "torn asunder" by Jesus, allowing that higher frequency of Spirit energy to work in human consciousness when we center our thoughts on Spiritual ideas.

All three Gospels make it clear that Jesus has come to fulfill a plan that has been in place throughout evolution. He tells His disciples of that plan and that it calls for His sacrifice. The following is one of His most profound statements concerning this:

John 6:39—"*and this if the will of him that sent me, that of all which he hath given me I should lose nothing; but should raise it up at the last day. For this is the will of my Father, that every one that beholdeth the Son and believeth on him should have eternal life.*"

The intention of the Father is that nothing will be lost in the sacrifice. In fact, it will be raised up after a period of adjustment. This is to say, that the atoms of His physical body will then function differently, in a higher frequency. All those that see this action in Jesus and believe in its possibility will have the same eternal life, following the necessary adjustment in consciousness. The will of GOD is eternal life and it has been the plan from the BEGINNING because GOD Life is unlimited and the plan is for it to be reflected into all realms of expression. The natural outworking of the law will produce this eternal life.

Jesus would show that death is not a reality, but merely a false belief, and that we who believe in death are "asleep." This is illustrated in the raising of the daughter of Jairus.

Matt.9:24—"*for the maid is not dead, but sleepeth*"

The belief that death is a reality and part of the plan is false. It is merely a "sleep" state of consciousness, not yet fully awake to the truth about life. This is again stressed in the raising of Lazarus. When Jesus was told that His friend, Lazarus, had died, He again said, "He is asleep." He deliberately waits "three days" before He goes to his tomb and calls him out, alive and well. The period of "three days" represents the time needed for all three aspects of the TRIANGLE principle of Life and Substance to transform physical atoms into spiritual Substance. Since all is taking place in Mind, the true LIGHT must adjust atoms in the physical, emotional, and mental fields of energy of the material plane and raise them to the spiritual plane. Jesus used the power of His vibrating words to raise Lazarus when He said, "Come forth Lazarus." Once again, we see the power of sound waves working to move and change the structures built by atoms.

This should not be hard to understand when we realize that certain rates of rhythm affect us. The rhythm of words move us with inspiration (in Spirit) when arranged in certain ways. This is why we are moved by poetry, prose, and sacred scriptures. Certainly the arrangement of musical tones and rhythms cause a great response in us. These examples are simply the manipulation and arranging of matter (atoms) which produce different effects in the electrical Mind and body of an individual.

TRANSFIGURATION

Jesus knew He was the LIGHT and He used this radiant energy as it was needed. A proof of this LIGHT within Him can be seen in the event of transfiguration. Jesus had taken three of His disciples, Peter, James and John apart from the others and onto a high mountain. This mountain can also simply mean that they were in an extremely high state of vibration when this event occurred. They saw Jesus transfigured.

Luke 9:28-36, "His countenance was changed and His rainment was white and glistening."

Matthew 17:1-13 and Mark 9:2-13 also tell of this experience, each describing shining rainment. It seems clear that they could see that the LIGHT was not being reflected by Jesus, but was coming from within Him with a "glory" that astonished them.

There appeared with him Moses and Elijah. Moses represents the law; Elijah the Prophets who insist upon living that law. Both of them had made their Ascension. They knew of the plan for the coming of Christ and the crucifixion. Jesus instructed His disciples to say nothing about this "vision" until after He had raised His body from the tomb. He clearly did not want to disperse, or spread out the wave of high energy within Him. What is this LIGHT? It is a wave motion of radiant energy and Jesus wanted to keep it focused within His mind, body and soul, to be used for His coming ordeal that would take place because of His love for humanity.

The teaching of Jesus Christ reveals that love produces a vibration of tranquility in the soul. This tranquil state of Mind and emotions should be the aim of anyone who desires to achieve a spiritual consciousness. This peace and tranquility was certainly demonstrated by Jesus when He carried out His mission. This kind of peace does not come through the effort of the personal will but through a response and recognition of the inherent vibration of the Christ within.

THE COSMIC PLAN

Let's get a picture of the great Cosmic Plan that is unfolding and was unfolding at the time of Jesus Christ and even before He made His appearance upon this planet. The healing of humanity is to take place so gradually that we sometimes believe that there is no healing going on, but it really is happening. Nothing happens by accident, we are not here by accident but we are all part of a great plan. Jesus taught in parable and symbol. He knew that it was important to observe rituals and this is evident when He tells the disciples to prepare an upper room at an Inn so that they may observe the Passover. He would use the Passover to initiate a new Covenant between GOD and mankind. The Feast of the Passover is filled with symbols which signify the destiny of mankind, the time when we will ultimately "pass over" from ignorance into illumination. Before Jesus, Moses had brought 600,000 Hebrews out of Egypt. The night before this exodus was called the "night of watching." It was later called the Passover.

The Israelites in Egypt were instructed to take the blood from an unblemished lamb and smear the blood of that lamb on the door of their house. They were to roast and eat the lamb with bitter herbs and unleavened bread. The lamb represents the perfected lower nature that is now innocent which will protect them and their household from death. The bitter herbs symbolize there suffering while in bondage in Egypt. Remembering that Egypt represents bondage to the material level of thought, the herbs represent a bondage to the flesh. The unleavened bread that contains no yeast for rising represents substance that has now been purified.

With their doors marked with the lamb's blood, the Israelites would escape the "angel of death" that would come upon the Egyptians (bondage). Their houses (consciousness) would be "passed over" and they would be led out of bondage by Moses.

How fitting that Jesus used the Passover as a symbol for the New Covenant which He would establish for humanity. Because of the events that were about to take place, the human race would be able to "pass over" from limited life that ended in death, into an awareness of eternal life. He used the bread to represent His body and the Wine to represent His Life blood.

METAPHYSICS AND PHYSICS
WORK TOGETHER

John 6:51-56 "*I am the living bread which came down out of heaven, that a man may eat thereof, and not die. If a man eat*

of this bread he shall live forever; yea, and the bread which I will give is my flesh, for the life of the world . . . Except ye eat the flesh of the Son of man and drink his blood, ye have not life in yourselves. He that eateth my flesh and drinketh my blood hath eternal life . . . He that eateth my flesh and drinketh my blood abideth in me, and I in him."

Needless to say, these words astonished those who gathered to hear Him speak! Of course, He is speaking symbolically but He is also speaking literally. The atoms of His flesh body will be "broken" and dispersed into the atmosphere of human consciousness and His blood will actually be "poured out" upon the energy field of material substance. This will change the frequency rate on the earth plane of human awareness since the atoms of His body were vibrating at the high frequency of the Cosmic Christ. This may seem impossible when we first hear this explanation, but is it really? Think a moment, of how amazing the idea of a radio broadcast would have been to the people of Jesus' time.

What is radio? The dictionary defines it as "a spontaneous decomposition of an atom resulting in radiation of three types and the formation of new substances."

Aha! When an atom is decomposed, it radiates! This radiation is of three types (there are three currents of energy in the triune principle of all creation) and this radiation forms new substances. Perhaps this is exactly what happened with the decomposition of the body atoms (bread) of Jesus and also with His life blood which was poured out for us. The radiation of these spiritualized atoms produced new 'waves' of energy patterns for humanity. They are electro-magnetic waves vibrating at a high frequency, just like radio waves, but they are vibrating at even a higher frequency than radio waves.

The currents of spiritual energy express as electricity on the earth plane. We use it all the time to transcribe and translate words and sounds in the telegraph and telephone. We no longer are amazed that speech can be transmitted by electrical currents moving over wires! We also now have wireless phones and computers, along with all sorts of electronic gadgets for messages and information. These are all transmitting thoughts around the globe.

How similar this is to the currents of Spiritual Energy that we saw

MOVING and expressing as GOD SAID in Genesis I. We are using natural physical laws and creative laws every day! How astonishing the idea of television would have been to the people of the Bible, but television is just an instantaneous transmission and reproduction of images through the medium of electrical impulses, or radio waves. This is the essence of creation! Genesis presents us with a picture of reproducing images as electrical impulses, or waves of energy, passing from one level of substance to another. Since everything takes place in Mind, it is plausible that consciousness of how this works individually will eventually be thoroughly understood by all of us.

We are able to discern and use light, which is a wave motion of radiant energy, as X-rays. The X-ray is radiation of such extremely high frequency that it has the property of passing through a solid. We must not forget that our dense physical bodies are also light waves in motion acting as electricity with the circuitry of the brain sending impulses throughout the body continually. The whole spectrum of light shows us seven bands of colored light rays, in the order of their wave lengths, which are all produced from the original white light as it separates into seven expressions. Therefore, we know there are still bands of light that we cannot yet use.

When Jesus said that He was the LIGHT of the world that shines in the DARKNESS, surely He was radiating these waves of energy at a very High frequency. In fact, He had to step down, or lower, the power that was at His disposal, because it would have been destructive on the material plane. This was His role as a transformer of the LIGHT. However, when He went to the cross, rose from the tomb, and ascended with the power of the higher frequency of LIGHT, He was allowing that power to fully work through Him.

Science has also taught us that light refracts, or bends, deflecting its radiation as it moves through substances of different densities. The physical body, as dense material substance, is surrounded by spheres of energy, or bodies, which can receive the whole spectrum of radiating LIGHT that Jesus Christ anchored on the material plane. This is the reason for communing with spiritual ideas (LIGHT).

Jesus presented the bread and wine as symbols to be appropriated and claimed by those who would follow Him in the regenerative process for the body. Through appropriating spiritual truth, we feed the Mind, and what is held in Mind will express through the body. This is the new Covenant that Jesus gave to mankind. It is the establishment of higher frequencies of LIGHT WAVES upon the material plane that can be contacted and used for "food" and "drink" for the consciousness of the human race.

GOING TO THE CROSS

Once we understand the science of Jesus we know Him as one who was fully awake to His identity as a Son and Sun (Light) of GOD. He knew the law of Being; that whatever He held in His Mind would manifest. He knew the Divine Plan from its very BEGINNING to its fulfillment and knew that it was His mission to reveal that Plan to mankind. He was one who had DOMINION over all He surveyed and was not disturbed by appearances of the physical plane. He was the Master of all Masters! Is this a compatible image with the traditional Christian image of a man who comes to the cross as a victim of betrayal and one who had lost control over the circumstances of His life? Certainly not!

Jesus had not been mistaken about His mission or about how it would be carried out. There was not anything more powerful that could have dominion over His consciousness, but traditional Christian teaching sends mixed messages. The Bible shows us that Jesus was clairvoyant and that He had no problem in knowing where people were in consciousness. It was easy for Him to see the source and cause of any situation. This ability would make it difficult to believe that He could be betrayed by one of His faithful disciples. It is also puzzling to justify that Judas, who sat at the feet of his Master for three years, receiving secrets that were only given to a few, could go against any of His Master's wishes. It seems impossible and not probable. Perhaps there is another way to think about this.

Jesus says over and over that He has come to fulfill the prophecy of the Old Testament and He quotes that Testament constantly. He knew that those who would search the scriptures would see the Plan and He came to fulfill that Plan. He knew that every action of His was leading Him to the cross. This is where He wanted to go! As already discussed, He was ready to strike the harmonious chord between the higher and lower vibrations of energy and there was no reluctance on His part to carry this out. His sacrifice would show mankind that it would be necessary for them to blend their outer, physical self with their inner spiritual Self, in order to be in harmony with the Plan of regeneration. Jesus wanted to show us how to be a "giver." Can one truly be a "giver" if trapped or betrayed into being a "giver'? No one can truly give unless they willingly want to give; otherwise, it is not a gift. Jesus gave without restraint, through a complete sacrifice of Himself.

The popular belief is that Judas betrayed Jesus because He wanted Him to set up a worldly kingdom and he wanted to force His hand to bring this about. That is not easy to accept, since one who lived so closely with Jesus would have known better than to think Jesus could be manipulated in this way. Jesus had told them many times about the Plan and that it was His mission to carry it out. Jesus purposely frightened the religious leaders with His teachings, so that they would want do away with Him and going into Jerusalem for the Passover Feast would put Him right where He wanted to be. Here, He would make the great demonstration and declaration of GOD'S eternal life for every human soul.

Jerusalem would be crowded with about a million people at Passover time. They would come to bring their sacrificial unblemished lambs to be slaughtered and burnt as offerings by the Priests of the Temple. He would offer Himself up as the unblemished lamb for the people and the symbolic meaning would be recognized down through the ages.

How was He to get to the cross? The religious and political leaders would have to know where He was and they would have to take Him at the right time, so that He could come to the cross before the Sabbath. He would need help from someone He could trust. This would be Judas, who was the treasurer of the group of disciples. His assignment would be to tell the Jewish leaders how they could arrest Jesus without interference from the crowds of people that always surrounded Him. At the celebration of the Passover Supper Jesus told the disciples that one of them would betray Him. They wondered who it would be.

He replied, **"I know whom I have chosen, that the Scripture might be fulfilled. (John 13:18) He it is to whom I shall give a sop."**

It was a tradition at the supper, to dip the unleavened bread in a paste made of apples and pomegranates and then into the bitter herbs. The paste represented the mortar used for building with bricks while the Israelites were in Egypt and the bitter herbs symbolized of the bitter bondage of slavery. The host would then present the sop to an honored and respected guest at the table. The sop was given to Judas. It does not seem likely that Jesus would have used this symbol to show his respect for Judas if He knew he was working against Him. It is more likely that Jesus had asked for his help and trusted His friend.

When giving the sop to Judas, Jesus said **"Go quickly and do what thou must do."**

After the supper Jesus withdrew to a Garden to pray and prepare Himself for the coming ordeal. Judas came with officers to arrest Him.

Jesus greeted him saying, **"Friend, why do you come?"**

Of course He knew why he had come, but addressing Judas as his friend, and showing surprise was Jesus' way of identifying Himself to the guards as the one whom they sought and by the question, they would not suspect that this was planned by Jesus. If the plan was to be fulfilled, it must appear that Jesus was taken by surprise. Thanks to His "friend" they were able to find Him and arrest Him. All had gone according to plan! The part Judas played in this plan was a great sacrifice on the part of Judas. He would bear the stigma of one who had betrayed the Christ!

THE SUFFERING CHRIST OF TRADITIONAL CHRISTIANITY

Through centuries, the Church and most Biblical Scholars have taught that Jesus felt that GOD had forsaken Him. This simply cannot be true, if we understand the consciousness of GOD in which He dwelt. He was well prepared for the crucifixion after His visit to the Garden of Gethsemane. He knew He was the instrument through which the Cosmic Christ worked to raise the human perspective to high enough levels whereby they could be released from their bondage and the fear of death. There was no fear in Jesus Christ, or He could not have achieved His goal.

Yet, He did cry out from the cross, *"My God, my God, why hast Thou forsaken me?"*

Jesus often quoted from the Old Testament writings. Here, He was quoting directly from Psalm Twenty Two. He was still teaching, even as He hung upon the cross. Psalm Twenty Two describes not only the details of the crucifixion but also the revealing of Jesus's whereabouts to the Priests. The crucifixion was a fulfillment of the Prophesies of old and Jesus wanted that to be understood by those who would follow Him. This quote from the Old Testament was a symbol for suffering humanity as they progress through their evolution; often feeling forsaken by God. The scripture tells how we will overcome these fears and merge with Reality of eternal life. Mind over Matter was demonstrated by Jesus!

The Christ was not crucified on the cross. Only the human belief in death was sacrificed. The Christ cannot be crucified because in Christ there is only eternal life with no interruption of death. Jesus showed us that death is only a belief held in human consciousness. That belief exists there because of all the fears and uncertainties that came as a result of a separation in Mind between GOD and human condition. Human fears and uncertainties were symbolically crucified on the cross by Jesus. These fears are the "sins" of mankind that must be given up. Jesus hung upon that cross to signify that Mind has DOMINION over matter. When the Mind is cleared of false beliefs as to who and what we are, eternal life will be our reality.

Jesus told us to follow Him. First we must follow Him in the regeneration of our thought and feeling and then we too, will be transformed and be ready for translation from a human being to a spiritual being. Do you remember the Einstein's discovery that matter can be turned into light and light can be turned into matter? This is the demonstration Jesus made. This is possible for us because it is the Law! Now we must do our part. Jesus came to show us how to save ourselves from fears that bind us. Shall we follow Him?

Just think of it! What a sacrifice it must have been for Jesus, who had risen from the material consciousness and experienced

life on the Solar plane to descend into the material plane of humanity. Thankfully, there are those who want to serve mankind so profoundly that they are willing to sacrifice in such a way to guide us along the path to Spiritual Freedom. This surely is the purity of God love that is willing to do this. The more we understand about Creation, its levels of MIND, with Its Infinite capacity for expression, the more we can love and appreciate Jesus. He truly points the way for us. We know He is still working for us because He told us it was His assignment to "bring all the sheep into the fold." What can we do to help in that assignment? We can begin by recognizing our own Divinity and then serving in our own particular way to help others find their way out of bondage to the material into the freedom of the Spiritual realms.

While so engaged, we must continually bring new insight to how we are using the God energy that empowers us, so that we shall always make selfless choices. It is a tremendous assignment but one that brings joy! We can always recall the words of Jesus when He said, "I will lose nothing." Truly, there is nothing to lose, only fulfillment to be gained.

Chapter 10

WHO ARE YOU?

I t is interesting that when we talk about the physical body we say, "my" body, or "his" body, or "her" body, or "this" body, or "that" body. We never talk about the body without showing ownership. Intuitively, we know that the body "belongs" to us and that we are not the body. Actually, the physical body is a point of contact in the physical world for the idea of body. If we were to surgically search the body for this idea it could not be found. The body is only the manifest form of an idea. Ideas live in Mind and Mind is outside of the space-time realm of being. Genesis tells us that there is only One Mind and that we all have consciousness in that One Mind. Therefore, the realm of Infinite Ideas is always available to us.

It is also interesting that when we ask the question "Who are you?" we use the verb "are." Normally, "are" indicates the plural, and is used with subjects such as "they," "those" and "these," while the word "is" indicates the singular. Have you always thought of yourself as singular? Of course, you have. That is because there is an idea of separation in your consciousness. You have believed you are separate from GOD and separate from others. This is the result of becoming conscious of your existence as "I AM": First, it was the Cosmic Christ that had this realization of personal identity at the Solar, or shall we say, the spiritual level. Because that Cosmic One has become many, every offspring of that Christ also has a personalized identity. What we have not yet discerned is that we simultaneously have both personal identity and spiritual awareness of being One. These two identities exist together but the physical is obvious and the spiritual is not. Do we intuitively realize that we are plural and not singular? That could explain why we ask the question, "Who are you?' and not, "Who is you?" You are much more than you appear to be. The science of Genesis and the Science of Jesus Christ make it clear that human beings must turn their thinking around and see themselves differently.

You have been looking at yourself from UNDER and not from ABOVE the WATERS, which are the potential Substance for forms. Remember, Jesus told the people, "*You are from beneath and I AM from above, you are of this world; I am not of this world.*" He also said *"My Kingdom is not of this world."* His Kingdom is a Kingdom of ideas and not of physical, material things. He proclaims, *"The Kingdom is within you!"*

BODY SCIENCE

When you see life from "UNDER," you start with the body. Let's look at that body in a scientific way. Physical Science is the ordered and systematic knowledge gained by experiment, induction, and observation. Your body is busy doing all of these all the time. Science teaches us that everything in the world of matter is made up of atoms and there is a formula for making all forms.

- If we start from the beginning of the physical world, we find electrons, which are the basic units of negative electricity. They associate with a positively charged nucleus to form an atom. Please note the dual currents of energy at work here, negative magnetism and positive radiation. It is Genesis all over again! Here is the TRIANGLE at work. Actually, science tells us that the chemical and physical properties of matter are determined by the action and grouping of electrons.

- An atom is a minute particle which is spheroidal in form. It contains within itself a nucleus of life which could be described as fire energy, or heat. Within it are molecules, the tiny units of energy, which in their totality, form the atom itself but the atom is mostly space. The activity of the atom is rotary motion, along with the ability to discriminate and develop. We have believed we are solid and dense matter, but we are also space. Perhaps we are actually living more in space that is not familiar to us than our earth bound space-time concept of existence.

- MAN is an aggregation of atoms and is also in a spheroidal form, with a nucleus of life at the center. This nucleus is the permanent atom of every individual which has been "mirrored" as a reflection of the Christ Self permanent atom, the "I AM." Just as in a hologram, each individual unit of the Christ Self contains the whole. All atoms of the lower bodies (fields of energy) are animated by the individual's life activities and the "will-to-be." They all vibrate according to the point reached in evolution by the individual.

- Therefore, MAN is a rotating sphere of matter with three essential characterizations:

- First, there is inertia at the BEGINNING. It is a state of quiescence for the "fire" energy in the permanent atom because there is not yet any stimulation from an aggregation of atoms. As Genesis would put it, there has not yet been a MOVING by SPIRIT (wind) ACROSS THE FACE OF THE WATERS. (Do you remember that WATER means Substance?)

- Next, AND GOD MOVED which causes the inherent fires of matter to produce enough heat to begin rotary movement. Eventually, this rotation results in radiation. This happens because of the dual nature of heat within matter which then affects other atoms in its environment. This interaction causes repulsion and attraction. This in turn produces a coherence of form and "bodies" of atoms come into manifestation.

- Next, rhythms with their vibrations produce wave frequencies. A point of balance must be achieved between these frequencies and this is the goal for the energies of life. This balance will occur when there is a unification of the three "fires," or levels of heat of the Creative TRIANGLE. A continual rotary, spiraling, cyclic, onward progression produces interaction of the inherent fires. When perfect balance is reached, the soul occupying the form will be released from the body. The electrical body of atomic matter has served as a tool for gaining experience.

It, along with material forms, has been a battleground of pairs and opposites so that choices could be made which served to expand the consciousness of the individualized "I AM" (soul).

Many years ago the poet, James Dillet Freeman, wrote the following verse after hearing Charles Fillmore, the Founder of the metaphysical movement, Unity, teach a class. It was one of the very first poems ever sold by this poet, who later had one his poems taken to the moon by astronauts. It speaks of the fiery presence of Spirit active in and around us.

SEA-STUFF

I live in an electric sea that flashes in and over me

Electric is the solid ground, its particles like bubbles bound,

Electric the transparent air, rivers of fire flow everywhere,

Too vast, too luminous for sight, the momentary shape of motion, A dazzling, dancing, living ocean, heaven and earth are not enough

I am myself this strange sea stuff.

It should be helpful here to mention the book that I read many years ago titled "Stalking the Wild Pendulum, the Mechanics of Consciousness" by Itzhak Bentov. He suggests that we swing back and forth like a pendulum of a clock between space-time and other dimensions. As a pendulum oscillates there is a state of rest before each direction change. He posits that we swing in consciousness several times per second, moving from the physical level, through velocities of the astral, mental and causal intuitive levels, and even to the state of "rest" that is the Absolute. At this level we experience omnipresence and are one with all creation. This constant reciprocal action from the lower to the higher and the higher to the lower is refining and awakening human consciousness.

This is plausible. Consider the original TRIANGLE of energies and see the Absolute-all knowing Mind at the apex with the Life idea (LIGHT) swinging like a pendulum to the opposite Substance idea (DARKNESS). Our consciousness is moving from the apex point of the TRIANGLE (Absolute), to the perfect Life idea, then into Substance which gives it form and back again to the Absolute. This reciprocal action could be going on all the time and yet, we are unaware of its activity.

SCIENCE OF THE PLAN

We have been exploring both physical science and spiritual science and it is clear that "as above, so below" and that the Cosmic Scheme is to bring HEAVEN AND EARTH together. We are on the material plane to help bring these two states of consciousness into perfect balance with each other.

All this brings speculation about many things concerning our future, including personal ascension. Ascension is possible for those who know how to use the universal energy of radiation and magnetism correctly. There is much to learn as yet, about these invisible forces of Mind. Jesus said we would do wondrous things because He knew that evolution would bring the capability to overcome the last enemy, which is the belief that death is inevitable. We can begin right now to reprogram our thoughts regarding the truth about Life and Substance. Everything, even the idea of eternal life is now within the grasp of human consciousness. Everything is first an idea before it is expressed, and knowing this, we can take that idea and let it grow, just as the symbolic, tiny mustard seed grows.

We are the offspring of the GOD SEED and the creation story is being played out through us. We can't ever be alone because we are the individualized "I" that is first and foremost the whole. Neither can we be without Life and Substance because they are our very essence. The power of reproduction is ours, so yesterday or today is not our limit, but in tomorrow is always infinite possibility. We don't know how long it will take to change our Mind about the idea of death and cast it out of the thought stream of humanity. However, we have learned a great deal that can help us achieve our goal.

SCIENCE OF PRAYER

Our study of Genesis and the mission of Jesus Christ present us with much food for thought because the subjects discussed are deep, but careful reading and quiet self-reflection should bring an intuitive realization of GOD within. You might ask, "If GOD is not "out there," but is the very energy within me, then to whom do I pray?" "Is prayer useful; does it really affect anything?" The answer would have to come as another question. The Bible has given you the formula for creation. It does not deny you a GOD. It just tells you that GOD is in Mind and acts as the Absolute Source of energy through universal laws. What a grand place for GOD to be! GOD could not be more personal than to be the very energy of your thoughts!

How do we pray? We use scientific prayer. We know that both thought and feeling are energy. Why not practice bringing these two together? Let's consider them as HEAVEN and EARTH. We can use visualization and imagination to picture the energy between these two flowing in reciprocal action. Scientific study has proved that the heart does more than pump blood through our body. The brain is important but the heart is the first organ formed. Our heart signals our brain what we feel to our brain. The brain signals our dual nervous system in accordance with those feelings. The brain, although sending the heart thoughts, must act according to what we feel. The heart has a choice what to feel about the thoughts sent by the brain, but not so with the brain, it must obey the heart.

This is the reciprocal action, described in Genesis in a moving figure eight pattern. The connection between the brain and the heart is essential to our ascension into higher planes of consciousness. The heart is our feeling nature and it has been discovered that when the feeling reaches 0.1 cycles per second an expanding field of energy forms around our body. Physicists tell us that the electromagnetic field of the heart is 5,000 X stronger than the brain's electromagnetic field. Through instruments, this field can be seen.

Scientists have shown that our heart is key to tapping into the Zero-Point energy that is the Substance out of which everything is produced. They have accepted that there is an all pervading Substance beneath the Quantum level that is the beginning of all creation. We must conclude that in the center of our heart there is an anchor attaching us to the Zero-point unlimited energy field.

This is the law of Genesis! The underlying Substance is the Divine feminine of the TRIANGLE and because of its powerful magnetism it receives ideas of life from the brain. This must be the Divine Substance (EARTH) that underlies everything. It acts as the matrix or womb to birth a form for the Life idea.

Do you remember our discussion of a hologram? We saw how a laser light is split and then projected through triangular mirrors onto a photographic plate, which in turn projects a mirrored image in mid-air of the object on that plate. It seems real (solid and of dense matter) but is only a reflection of the object on the plate, not the object itself. The object on the plate was an image just like an image we hold in our mind through brain power. However, if we have indifferent feelings without appreciation in our heart about the image, it will not manifest because there must be interference between two light beams. This is the duality of the TRIANGLE law. That is why sending love from our heart to the brain about any given subject is vitally important. What will be produced depends upon what kind of feeling we are projecting onto the image plate of mind.

As you lift your thoughts to the spiritual nature of love, along with a willingness to discard any selfish thought, you release the situation to the natural outworking of the law, which is wholeness. Selfish thoughts block the full force of GOD'S pure energy, just as personal concern presents fears that inhibit the natural flow of wholeness. Scientific prayer is prayer without fear. It is an affirmation of GOD Presence and Power. It is the invoking of Spiritual activity through the power of the word. GOD will overcome, overpower anything as long as you are willing to surrender to that Power and accept the will and intention of GOD, as opposed to your own. You will give yourself through the love you have for GOD. You can easily say, "Thy will be done loving Father-Mother GOD" when you know that GOD is the love that freely gives without impediment when you get yourself out of the way.

In order to do this, you must work with your consciousness regarding who and what you are. The way you see yourself is the key to demonstrating the goodness of GOD in your world. If you are mistaken about your identity and see limitations, your feelings about these thoughts will affirm that for you by presenting them in your life. Adversely, if you see only the power of a Self-giving GOD, that awareness will also be demonstrated in your life. Learn to invoke the Power within and direct Its force. It is there to be used and manifested! See yourself as you really are; an expression of God's Love. It takes practice to train your thoughts and give yourself away, so why not start today?

Remember always, that Deity does not pour out Its energy upon a waiting world! Instead, it is latent within the world itself, just as energy is latent within the atom. This GOD energy is driving you on toward a goal, just as the current in a river drives the boat through water. The trick is not to go against the current! Learning the truth of your being and how the law works through you can unlock and release the powers that lie within yourself. You do not have to draw GOD into any situation, GOD is already within it!

You can use your imaging power to see GOD "glorified" and "radiating" within you, or any other person or condition, when you live in your heart. Prayer does work! When an unwanted appearance occurs, choose to change your Mind about it and see the good there. Picture the underlying Substance of Wholeness that lies hidden invisibly in it. Imagine the infinite ocean of Substance that is all-good and see it being drawn into the condition to overcome any appearance. Hold this Truth in your heart, love it, and soon you will see results! Your focus of attention must be to feel that GOD love in your own heart while commanding your brain to image what you feel. We cannot argue or reason with illness but we must dare to choose love that is all powerful because it is GOD itself. Metaphysics teaches that we must forgive ourselves for error committed and accept and love ourselves. Only then are we able to truly love others. Loving the GOD within you is the key to loving yourself and others.

Jesus was the fullness of love expressed in the world. He told us we are supplied with all we need, the same as Him. Now that we have more understanding of the formula of LIFE Itself, we can learn to work in the "fields" of energy joyously producing a harvest of perfection. It is already within us. Now we know where not to look for GOD, we have always thought we were separate from GOD but we are ONE.

I invite you to prove this to yourself. Remember that Genesis taught us that GOD said, "LET THERE BE LIGHT." That is to say, let there by awareness or a consciousness of what exists. Since there was nothing yet except the TRIANGLE It had to look at Itself. In order to do this It had to turn Itself inside out! had to look within You can see what happens as a result by taking a sock and turning it inside out. Yes, go get a sock and see what happens when you turn it inside out. It is inverted! The toe that was at the top is now at the opposite end. This is just what happens when we look in the mirror. Recall the inverted TRIANGLES pictured in this book. This inversion also shows up as the triangles invert again and again through self-reflection, to make a wave of energy. This wave of triangular energy causes a crisscross flow like the letter "X." This is the hologram principle and also the DNA Structure. The TRIANGLE also expresses as the pattern for the human body, one inverted above the other and the body itself is made up of many TRIANGLES. These TRIANGLES are the framework for the body which is really a thought form produced by mind and heart action.

The time is now ripe for many to enter into a new thought sphere that is a higher expression of love than this humanity as yet to express. Many have discovered the action of the Holy Spirit within and have been guided by that love. The only thing that holds us back is the belief that brain power is more important than love power. From this day forward let yourself live in your heart's natural love. This is where the tremendous power works to bring about positive change and it will move us into a new vibration where we will be able to experience a different kind of reality.

Many trained in Science, Math and Philosophy have written books that explain in detail some of these ideas. Greg Braden tells us that it is a scientific fact that every 5,000 years the planet Earth goes through an inversion, or reversal, of its magnetic field. Scientists say we are in the process of that at the present time. We are about to enter into a new vibratory frequency that will produce a new kind of world for us. The heartbeat of the Earth is changing its rhythm. Our planet has speeded up and every cell in our bodies is trying to keep up with this new pattern of energy. The pulse of our planet is twice the beat that it was in the 1980's. Our beliefs will change to match the new beat. Braden says that we will know that we can create different kinds of feelings from those of the past. Our heart is a field of energy that connects us to the energy of the Earth. The power of human emotion is in our heart but is connected to the LOVE substance that is below the Quantum level. It is unlimited and all powerful.

Another writer, Drunvalo Melchizedek reminded me of the program NOVA produced several years ago, telling us that Science predicts the poles of our planet will reverse because the magnetic field around the Earth is weakening. This magnetic field encircles the Earth but is now being drawn into the Earth at the top of the globe. It is going into the heart of the planet instead of staying without. Seems to me, that this is just what we must do. We must draw our magnetic field of love energy within to know it is our true nature. We have felt separated from it, but not so, we are love because we are a mirror reflection of GOD whose nature is love. This will cause a reversal of thought and erase hate, fear, and doubt from our heart and brain so that magnetic natural love may be expressed through us. The fact is that when we feel love, loved, and loving, we become that love.

Who are you? You have evolved enough to know with certainty that you are not your body, but you have provided yourself with a body to experience on the material level. You know where not to look for GOD. You must "turn" to seek God within and little by little you shall see the fullness of the LIGHT within the DARKNESS. Now you are moving in the right direction. It is for each soul to find the LIGHT and each must find the Kingdom within in their own way. Then will come opportunities and responsibilities to ascertain the true from the false in all things. Goodness and holiness arise out of self-realization of your own holiness. Holiness is not your personality; it is your true Self, your real identity, the eternal Christ.

May you live wisely, act with kindness, speak words of harmony and healing, and practice self-forgetfulness. May your objective be to release the imprisoned Splendor of the Christ within yourself so that EARTH may receive HEAVEN.

May you pray in the same manner as Jesus in John 17:4, ***"Father, glorify thou me, with thine own Self, with the glory which I had with Thee before the world was."*** This is not a selfish prayer, but an act of invoking GOD energy to radiate Its power into the personal self. In so doing, prayer is not to confine GOD to the personal self, but to spread GOD'S glory throughout the world for the ultimate recognition of the unity between GOD and MAN.

Today, it is heartening to hear that some scientists are saying that the DNA actually produces genes that are programmed to seek spiritual understanding. Truly, mankind is evolving to a greater awareness of its origin and destiny. It is time to be alert to the prodding from within so that the LIGHT of Spirit may shine in all Its glory!

A few simple rules are helpful:

- Deny that any negative appearance has power within itself. The power is within you and you can change your Mind anytime you choose.
- Affirm the Truth, regardless of appearances and hold to that truth until you see the outer condition change.
- Invoke the power from within and decree that it is NOW acting to produce harmony, regardless of appearances. You need not ask, your needs are already known, claim the activity of GOD is at work in every situation as you change your consciousness about it. This is what Jesus meant when He prayed, "forgive us our debts, as we have forgiven our debtors."
- Never allow yourself to believe that you are a miserable, unworthy sinner, deliberately disobeying GOD. You are working out your evolution and this is exactly what you were born to do.

OUR MINDS ARE MADE FOR STRETCHING

A quotation from Thoreau seems appropriate here, "To him whose elastic and vigorous thought keeps pace with the sun, the day is a perpetual morning." Thoreau's adjectives for thought, "elastic and vigorous" are well chosen. Stretching present mental capacity in search of life's meaning and purpose is what makes existence interesting and valuable. Through the power of Mind anything and everything is constantly renewed and we are programmed for continual renewal through cyclic changes. Since the sun in our solar system is but the reflection of even a greater LIGHT, it is undergoing constant change and so are we.

With this in Mind, it is not impossible to believe that our planet may undergo a change in orbit, just as the little particle of Quantum physics changes orbit. This would produce another vibratory pattern which could bring much needed insight to the human race. Like any other organism in the universe, we are unfolding in stages, and as we do, greater powers flow in and through us. Creation and evolution are not separate nor are they in conflict with each other. They are both an operation of Mind, impregnating invisible Substance with invisible Life ideas, which become visible matter that is animated by the energy within it. Every idea has infinite possibilities for expression because the BEGINNING and CREATION is always happening. This view of life should help us recognize the intrinsic value of everything that happens to us and through us.

To understand evolution, is to recognize vibration and the response to vibration as the "forces" behind evolution. The science of the creation story has shown us that it is the energy of Mind that is active on both the inner and outer planes as vibrating radiation and magnetism. Our brain is radiating ideas of life and our heart is magnetic so they can be manifested. This is the activity that builds forms in many dimensions. This helps us understand the words of Jesus when He said, ***"In my Father's House there are many mansions."*** We have seen how intelligence exists within every facet of creation from the Solar level to the activity below the atom, which is called Quantum Mechanics and even below that to the plane of all-pervading Substance. In the great Cosmic evolution we seek to make practical application of the truth we know so that we may consciously further the innate plan of the GOD SEED.

Scientists once thought the atom was the ultimate particle, that is to say, the lowest level of matter, but now they know that at the center of the atom is a force that is a phase of electricity. This center of energy is active with its own internal makeup which radiates heat within the atom. Scientists found even smaller bodies, than that of electrons circling round the positive nucleus. Now they have found that underneath the space in the atom, below the quantum level, is boundless Substance. The atom is a microcosm of the Solar system. It seems the atom is the mirrored reflection of the original GOD SEED and it acts like a seed in that it gives its properties of Life by entering into the infinite, unlimited Substance that is all pervading everywhere in our universe. The magnetic energy of Substance is always here for us to use. Surely, Jesus referred to that availability when He said, "the Kingdom of Heaven is at hand." How good it is to know the law of Creativity and how it works. This should give us the confidence required to be utilize our God given powers.

Can you imagine yourself as something other than a physical human made of matter? How about a body of LIGHT? The material body has served us well but will we always need such a body? Jesus showed us that body matter can be changed into LIGHT. It is just as Einstein said, light can become matter and matter can become light. Why not place an image of a LIGHT body on the photographic plate of your brain and let your heart love it every day?

THE STRING THEORY

We have explored the possibility of linking science with the theology of Genesis and the analogy would not be complete without including the new theory of science that many physicists are working with today. They say they are searching for the "Holy Grail" in their exploration of the "String Theory." Brian Greene, author of the book, "The Eloquent Universe" presents this theory and what follows is my simplified explanation.

Some Physicists today believe the entire universe is made of tiny vibrating strings of energy. According to their particular vibration, they are shaped into patterns and these patterns are the "stuff" of structure and form. Albert Einstein gave us the theory of Relativity with its certainty and probabilities, and this solves the mystery about big things like galaxies and planets, but it does not explain the nature of tiny things like the protons and neutrons of the atom. Now we also have the Quantum level of things with its uncertainties of predictability. The two theories, one of certainty, the other of uncertainty, (Relativity and Quantum) conflict with each other. Science is searching for something that unites the two. Could the "String Theory" be the one single law that can bring the two together, so that we can understand both the big things and the tiniest things?

The "String Theory" says that at the heart of every particle of matter is a vibrating string of energy. They are so tiny that they cannot be seen and therefore are not testable and cannot be proven by observation or experimentation. Physicists believe this string of energy can contract, wiggle, and move itself into shapes just as the string of a violin can be made to sound different notes according to how it is touched with the bow and finger of the violinist. This string in the particle vibrates different notes or frequencies which produce mass and charge. Here is the electric universe at a level so deep that it cannot be seen.

This theory was not taken seriously at first because it suggested that there must be other dimensions. However, after years of working calculations, physicists have proved that the theory is free from anomalies. The theory has the mathematical depth to accommodate all four forces known to physicists, which are gravity, electro magnetism, weak forces and strong forces. Scientists have shown that gravity exists even at the string, quantum level. Gravity has a unifying quality just like love. In that case, it seems that love exist at the string.

Now science is entertaining the existence of other dimensions. This would affirm that there is much more than we can observe here in the dimension of space-time. Perhaps science is upon the threshold of finding the "Holy Grail." The "String Theory" has been called the Theory of Everything. Could this string of energy, believed to exist in the tiny BEGINNING of everything, be the same wiggling, moving energy found in the GOD SEED of Genesis I? Dare to believe what both Genesis and science is telling us.

WHO ARE YOU?

The Holy Grail will never be found in the material, physical world. When Jesus said at the Last Supper "drink this cup in remembrance of me, it is my blood poured out for you." He was speaking of Cosmic Consciousness. He invites us to partake of that Christ Life realm of MIND and feel it with our heart. You are a cup of consciousness that is called the Holy Grail and it is waiting for you to wake up!

Who are you? You are a unit of Christ energy that is at present, expressing a particular level of consciousness as a human being, but you are part of a colossal whole. You are like the hologram, in that you contain the whole and therefore can evolve to the point of producing a full expression of that whole. When Jesus prayed in the Garden before His crucifixion, He said, *"I am in you, you are in me, we are in them, and they are in us"* (John 17). Here we see His understanding that GOD is all in all.

If we be Spirit, we know that Spirit can break out of any confined limitation and eventually transcend its present form for one more suited to Its need. Looking at nature, we see that when there is to be change, crystallization occurs, which is then broken up and new life appears. When our old ideas become stagnant, either in Science, Philosophy, or Religion, spiritual fire energy will break up that crystallized form and take on new form. Watch for these new forms and be ready to stretch your Mind and entertain new concepts of life and love. Understanding the TRIANGLE can change mankind. It is essential that the old concepts of God be erased because they are limited. These limiting beliefs are behind all negative conditions and suffering of mankind. Whatever one thinks about God motivates his actions. It is time to grow up! I am reminded of Paul's words, "When I was a child I thought as a child." Humanity has come of age. It is time for great changes to take place.

We are used to seeing changes in governments because consciousness demands it. Presently we are undergoing changes in religious beliefs, so that the Church as we have known it in the past will no longer exist. Instead, the future holds beliefs of a more scientific and sectarian view of life, and is seeking a deeper understanding of the symbols of philosophy and religion. We must be willing to stretch consciousness from the material, to the universal, and even to the Absolute.

YOU are an essential part of the whole! The science of you is that you are a unit of energy that has sprung from the original One, which is the Cosmic Man, "The Only Begotten Son," which is called the Christ. You know yourself as a separate "I AM" and you possess the powers of independent thought and the spoken word. Your goal is to one day express Divine wisdom and perfect love in a unique way. You are learning how to do this by gradually releasing material beliefs and realizing new and higher ones. You are a co-creator with GOD, constantly radiating LIGHT and magnetizing new energy patterns to be filled and expressed. You are a mirrored reflection of the eternal Cosmic Christ.

YOU have been experimenting and expressing through matter, now it is time to move on to other more lofty activities. Attaining the next level of consciousness is not the ultimate, but it is the next evolutionary step in the vast expanse of Infinite Mind! You might ask, "When this present cycle is over, where will I be and what will I be doing?" No need to worry, for revelation comes as it is needed. Instead, your question really should be "Have I at last journeyed far enough to know that joy comes when I, just like a seed, willingly give my old identity away to become something new?"

The nature of GOD is hidden in the science of Genesis and the scientific contribution of Jesus Christ. The Bible says that fusion with all the attributes of God is your destiny because the nature of GOD. You are a seed produced from the original GOD SEED and you are steadily giving yourself away to become a Christ, a sun of GOD. What great news, the seed you are will produce that Self and with that event, the person that you believed you were, will merge with the Christ you really are!

Let us pray together:

Oh Christ, Thou Son of God, My own Eternal Self

Live Thou, Thy Life in Me, Do Thou, Thy Will in Me

Be Thou made flesh in me, I have no will but Thine

I have no Self but Thee, Oh Christ, Thou Son of God!

[Author unknown]

I would suggest that once you have recognized the sound of your inner voice don't hesitate to follow it regardless of what your outer self may think or what circumstances may seem to prevent you from following it. Listen and then trust that inner wisdom. My experience has been that it is the most reliable leading to follow. Let me give you an example.

After taking a year off to write a book about the Bible and with the book in the hands of a publisher, I had to make a decision of what to do next. I had returned to Dallas to write and in meditation asked inner wisdom for direction. The words came, "Go home!" I reasoned that I was home because I loved Dallas and considered it my home. Nevertheless, the voice repeated, "Go home!" Later that day I decided to call Unity Headquarters and talk to the woman who placed Ministers in Unity Churches. I told her I was ready to submit my resume to Churches looking for a new Minister. She responded at once with, "Aren't you from Cincinnati?" "Yes," I told her. She went on to tell me that a Church there was without a Minister for Good Friday and Easter and asked if I would be interested in going there. I knew about this little Church in downtown Cincinnati because I had visited it years ago with my teacher. Since my daughter lived in Cincinnati, it sounded like a good idea to try out for that Ministry. How could I refuse after my inner voice had told me to go home and this was indeed where I had spent most of my life?

No doubt my consciousness was going before me and preparing the way. I was asked by that Congregation to serve as their Minister. Now comes the most unexpected part of this story. They had been trying to sell their building for ten years and had not received one offer. However, they did have a good sum of money in the bank and I suggested that since we also owned a small lot next door, why not use it to build a new entry into the Church and also make the Sanctuary larger. I pictured an atrium with a fountain in the entrance. The Church was located in an area that was now being restored and rebuilt, which could bring new growth for us. There was a new Parking Garage just across the street which we could use on Sundays at no cost. With the Board's agreement, I was consulting with a building contractor in the lobby of the Church a few days later, when I was called to the phone. It was a Realtor. He said he had a cash buyer for our building who wanted to turn it into a restaurant. To make a long story short, we accepted the offer and had thirty days to vacate.

Meeting with the Board, we had to decide where we would relocate. One of the members said he knew just the place. It had been a nursery and had beautiful trees on five acres, along with a house. We went the next day to see it, paid cash, and began packing. We planned to hold classes in the house and also use it for office space until we could get the new Sanctuary built. In the meantime, we were able to use a nearby school auditorium for Sunday Services.

Hold on, that is not the real purpose in telling this story! It just so happened that the property we bought was located about a five-minute walk from the home where I had spent my married life with husband and children. It was in a neighborhood that I knew well. I was home! My inner voice had guided me ALL THE WAY home. Step by step, again I had been led to participate in activities that were even greater than I could have imagined. To build a Church is quite an adventure, but one that I cherish, and with the help of others I was able to enjoy a beautiful church home. It is still thriving and beautiful today.

Although I have been retired from my work with that Congregation for many years, I am aware that my work is not yet finished. At this writing, I continue to teach. I have been given many opportunities to share the insight I received about the symbols in the Creation Story of Genesis. It is truly like not being able to keep a secret. I just have to tell it! That inner voice still tells me what is best to do and presents new ideas all the time. There is no end to learning and awakening. It is my hope that you have great expectation for boundless good in your life and that you too will tell others about the secret TRIANGLE. As you listen to that quiet inner voice of wisdom, it will guide you in your particular service to mankind. God's Magnificent Plan is bringing you to the fulfillment of your joyous destiny.

Recently, I watched the movie made in 1981, called "Chariots of Fire." You may have seen it and know that it is a story about two champion runners. Their power to achieve their goal came from within themselves. It was the Fire of Spirit! These runners were Chariots of Fire! One of the young men had been told that his destiny was to become a Clergyman but he loved to run. He felt it was clear that his destiny was to become a champion runner. He dedicated himself to that goal and with hard work and discipline he achieved it. At the end of the movie we hear a statement made by him,

"I believe God made me for a purpose. He also made me fast. I will run for His glory!"

God has a purpose for you. Whatever you discover it to be, may you achieve it for God's Glory. Let the tremendous power of God be your guiding light. Just listen, listen, listen, all you need is already within you as fiery energy.

YOU TOO, ARE A CHARIOT OF FIRE!

FUSION

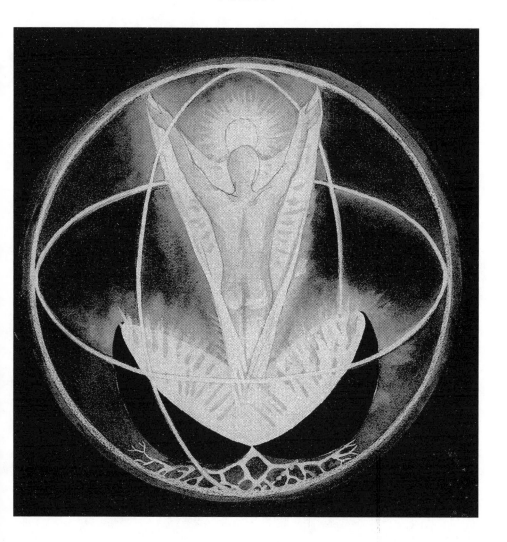

APPENDICES

ARCHETYPICAL MAN

In this book he is called the Cosmic Christ and Grand Man of our Solar System. It is the pattern, or imaged reflection, of the Absolute, which we call God. This Archetype is the World-soul (consciousness of perfection) that became complete at the end of the period of Involution, when Its qualities were fully immersed into the lower realms. Following this, the period of evolution began for the individualized consciousness, which is the soul. It embodies the perfection that exists in the Archetypal Man, but it must be gradually realized through long periods of time.

The soul, functioning on the lower plane, forms an Archetype, or pattern, as an image in consciousness, which will then be produced as material form. We can image an Archetype through our free will and therefore experience it.

The planes of Infinite MIND in our Solar System are as follows:

THE ABSOLUTE GOD

THE ARCHETYPICAL MAN

THE CELESTIAL PLANE—REALM OF LOVE

THE SPIRITUAL PLANE—REALM OF WISDOM

THE MENTAL PLANE—REALM OF BOTH HIGHER AND LOWER MIND

THE ASTRAL PLANE—REALM OF DESIRES

THE PHYSICAL PLANE-REALM OF EFFECTS AND SENSES

CAUSAL BODY

This represents the level of the higher mind. It is a storehouse for that which is worthy and true, suitable for eternal use. It is connected to the physical body and the temporary personality of the lower mind. It is at first potential only. It becomes an actuality through a process of building up, life after life, the qualities, virtues and Truths realized by the soul on the lower level. When perfected it forms the glorified body of Spirit. Metaphysically it is sometimes called the Christ body or the resurrected body. It can also be called the immortal soul.

In the story of Noah and the Ark it is symbolized as the Ark. Here is stored the virtues and qualities eligible to be preserved in this causal body. All that is not in this protective vehicle is washed away so that a new beginning can be provided for the soul.

It can also be understood as memory. The evolving soul can draw from this memory to rise in consciousness because all that is stored in the causal mind-body is that which is pure and eternal. In other words, all past development that expresses the vibratory rhythm of the higher realms is returned to the individual through ideas that come into the lower mind. When the soul achieves and beholds the Truth and acts with love and understanding, it is in harmony with the causal attributes and participates in Divine Wisdom.

Through a reciprocal flow of energy the lower and the higher feed each other. Eventually, the lower wishes to be drawn into union with the higher and at that point is consumed by the higher and then operates only in the spiritual realms.

Throughout this process both have had a consciousness of "I AM" and the causal body is the body being built as the eternal temple for the living God that experiences as the "I AM" on all levels of MIND. Without the causal body the soul would not progress and awaken, but instead have to remain ignorant of the powers within it. What has been sown in past lives will be reaped when it is needed and also at the so-called "harvest" of the God qualities.

CHRIST

Christ is not Jesus but existed as THE ONLY BEGOTTON SON at the dawn of creation. Christ is the offspring of God; a perfect reflection of all the attributes of God. Christ is the consciousness of perfection that sacrifices and disperses the Life and Substance of God MIND through individualization. Each individual possesses the perfection and wholeness from which it came. God is all in all.

Jesus, the embodiment of all the Divine ideas, demonstrated the invisible Power as consciousness ruling over matter. Therefore He is Jesus Christ who is not subject to the physical laws of the material plane. The word Christ means "Messiah" and "anointed one" which indicates supreme dominion and freedom from any limitations. Christ consciousness always knows "I AM," which is opposite from the human consciousness that questions "AM I?" When the quickening power of the "I AM" is recognized in the individual, the birth of Christ has taken place within and Truth begins to reveal itself.

The Bible calls the early expression of this Christ consciousness "Jehovah." This Old Testament Deity establishes spiritual law through Moses and the methods to practice it is taught through the Prophets and various other characters. The New Testament announces a new cycle beginning for humanity through the birth of Jesus Christ who symbolizes the birth of Christ within the human being. He told us to look within ourselves for God's Kingdom of ideas. This part of the Bible is understood according to the degree of awakening that has occurred in the individual.

Jesus showed us the Christ Consciousness can regenerate the body, resurrect it, and ascend the body into the higher spheres. He told His followers, "You will do even greater things than these which you have seen me do" and then instructed, "follow me, I AM the resurrection and the Life."

The last Book of the Bible, Revelation, introduces the end of human evolution when all will be able to ascend into the Kingdom of perfect ideas. We each are the "anointed one," we need only to wake up to that Truth.

To follow and abide in Christ is to consciously realize your unity with the Divine and with the Son (Christ), which is your own eternal self.

COLOR FREQUENCIES OF LIGHT

When the original TRIANGLE observes Itself, a mirror inverted image appears. Because of this duality manifestation can occur through Self-Reflection continually. With two TRIANGLES light can be reflected. This is the LIGHT of GOD, which is then passed through a lens called the FIRMAMENT where it refracts the LIGHT into seven light waves.

Each has a different vibration that is a quality. We speak of these vibrating light waves as realms, levels, dimensions, and spheres of activity in which the soul enters in order to develop that particular quality. Although we are familiar with the seven rays (days) in Genesis, there are really twelve presented in the Creation process. The other five are known esoterically as the secret rays. The soul development on these rays will come later in evolution because they function only on the higher levels and when humanity has awakened to the higher.

The seven added to the five total twelve. These twelve radiating and magnetizing frequencies are symbolized in the Zodiac as constellations through which the sun or LIGHT of the soul must pass. This passage of LIGHT in the Cosmos is mirrored in the soul on the lower level from incarnation to incarnation. This is an ancient Truth and is known in Religious Mystery Teachings worldwide. In *The Secret Triangle* the rainbow symbolizes humanity's attachment to this eternal LIGHT in the story of Noah in the Bible.

It is interesting that in the Lobby of the CIA Building in Washington D.C. a Zodiac is displayed from a large global ceiling fixture. The Library of Congress also displays it in its marble floor. One can travel the world and see the Zodiac everywhere. Christianity traditionally has not understood the Zodiac and its connection to humanity. Ancient Wisdom Teachings know that "As above, so below."

Many who profess a belief in the Bible do not know the Bible presents the signs and qualities of the Zodiac's twelve over and over again.

- 12 sons of Esau
- 12 Sons of Jacob

- 12 Tribes of Israel
- 12 Nations of Israel
- 12 flags of Israel, each symbolizing a quality
- 12 stones in the breastplate worn by Aaron and Israelite Priests
- 12 loaves of the shew-bread in the Tabernacle of the wilderness
- 12 spies sent out by Moses
- 12 stones to make an alter
- 12 stones taken out of the River Jordan
- 12 years of age when Jesus taught the Priests
- 12 Disciples with Jesus as the "SUN" in the center
- 12 gates John sees in Book of Revelation

The study of these qualities is taught in the Unity Movement from the book by its founder, Charles Fillmore, called *The Twelve Powers.* Theosophy also presents a thorough study through the Alice Bailey books.

Genesis shows how these qualities are immersed into the lower spheres and are called the seven "Days." They symbolize the seven Rays of vibrating waves of LIGHT involved in the Creation of mankind. Actually, there is no time as we know it on the higher realms, so we know the word is a symbol.

Auras can be seen around the body. They are the reflected radiation of the five light waves on the upper levels that are invisible to those using only the five senses. The aura radiates waves of the physical, emotional, lower mental, and etheric bodies (fields of energy). It is this radiation that an Initiate or Master watches and helps the student to achieve a balanced expression of desired virtues. The aura may not be visible to most people but its effect on those around a well-developed spiritual consciousness is enormous.

Since there is no time and space in Reality the sun never really enters any sign but it just appears to do so because we believe in the passage of time and the necessity of getting from one place to another. We see what our state of consciousness can imagine. Quantum physics and the

Bible both show that we choose what to see. There is the story about Galileo that applies here. When he had authorities of the time look through his telescope to show them mountains on the Moon, they could not see them and declared it a falsehood. Their consciousness could not accept the idea, so they could not see the Moon differently than they had always seen it. We are at present entering into another cycle that awaken us to more possibilities and will change what we choose to see. Cycle by cycle we are getting closer to choosing Reality.

DEATH

The fear of death has prevailed throughout human evolution but the physics of Genesis tells us that death of the old brings a new beginning. When consciousness of Reality is immersed into a material form death takes place but also brings a new beginning in the form state. When death of that form occurs it provides opportunity to change into a fresh form, much like changing any garment for another. At physical death the soul finds itself free from the restraints and bondage to a vehicle. We have changed garments many, many times and as long as our consciousness identifies with a material form that is the way we will experience life. When we know that we are soul and not the body, then we may focus consciousness on any plane we choose.

At physical death for the aspirant who knows the Truth of being, there is an immediate entrance into a sphere of service and expression to which he is well accustomed, which he recognizes and is accustomed to. This is because in his sleeping hours he had engaged in activities of learning and service in that particular sphere of activity. I remind you that Genesis shows us that *something cannot be made out of nothing*. What we are today molds what we are tomorrow and the same law functions in and through all spheres of consciousness. Also, Quantum Physics reveals that what we observe is what we choose to observe and that choice depends upon what we understand to be true.

The intention of the Absolute is for human beings to change garments at the demand of their own soul. Eventually, humanity will withdraw the soul from the physical body at will, leaving it behind. Without the light of the soul, the physical form will decay in the natural process and its atoms will pass back into the pool of waiting units to be used to form other incarnating souls. This happens according to the law of conservation that requires that nothing is wasted. It is through this law that the atoms of the physical body of Jesus were dispersed into the consciousness stream of humanity. These atoms have raised the vibratory frequency for human life wave.

One who understands the great Law of Life and Substance in the *Secret Triangle* should have no fear of death. It is simply the opening of another door into our chosen sphere of activity. We know through the Bible,

Ancient Wisdom Teaching, and the physics of Genesis that death is not God's way. Instead, we may choose to stay "awake" in the joy of union with eternal freedom from fear as we enter into consciousness of everlasting Life.

PRAYER

It is <u>Aspiration and supplication</u> of the lower to the higher. It is <u>asking</u> for a specific result. This is a state of mind that believes the result has to be sent and is conditional upon certain behavior or action.

<u>Affirmative prayer</u> realizes that the result already exists. <u>To decree</u> a result is <u>to invoke</u>, or draw forth, its appearance from the higher into the lower with confidence that it is already established. Therefore, to affirm and decree is stronger than faith in that it declares the Truth rather than the imperfect outer condition.

<u>Scientific prayer</u> is one of understanding that the Spiritual vibratory beat is harmonizing with the image placed in mind and felt in the heart and is already accomplished. Divine Wisdom and Perfect Love of the "I AM" erases error in consciousness so that what is imaged can appear.

<u>Devotional prayer</u> is the exercise of <u>adoration</u> for the presence of God. Devotion comes from the heart as a feeling of <u>love</u>. When this love is pure and innocent of selfishness there is a total <u>surrender</u> of the personal that draws the soul into higher vibrational frequency. This has been seen as light emanating from within the physical body. When devotion to the hidden splendor within is practiced on a regular basis an aura of light can be seen around the body as well as light from within the body.

<u>When asked how to pray, Jesus replied with all the above,</u>

Our Father—acknowledge God-seed is planted in MIND (Affirm Power Source of life)

Who art in Heaven—perfection exists as consciousness (devotion)

Hallowed be Thy name—Honor that perfection and link yourself with it (surrender)

Thy Kingdom Come—Ideas of perfection manifest (invoke)

Thy Will be done—will of God is perfect love (decree)

On Earth as it is in Heaven—unite imperfection with perfection (affirmative)

Give us this Day—eternal flow (affirm)

Our daily bread—Substance is unlimited (decree)

Forgive us our debts as we forgive our debtors—Law of cause and effect (scientific and decree)

Leave us not in temptation—world of desire (decree)

But deliver us from evil—seeing life from without (decree)

For Thine is the Kingdom, Power and the Glory—(devotion)

When praying watch your motive. Is it linked with love for God? Link yourself with that God Power at the start and affirm it is acting NOW. Decree and invoke the image you are picturing in mind is manifesting and be careful about the image you have formed in mind, whether it be for another or for yourself. See only the perfection you know is already there. It is God's pleasure to give! It is the nature of God to give! It is God's Law that responds to your prayer.

REINCARNATION

Successive embodiment of the soul enables it to gain experience through the evolutionary process. It provides opportunities for the development of spiritual qualities so that the lower may be perfected by the higher. The Bible alludes to reincarnation through symbolic events but barely mentions it throughout. That is because it is incidental to the development of the total Spiritual Plan. Just as sleep provides renewal for the physical body, re-embodiment provides renewal for a fresh intellectual outlook as well as a new body.

Just as it is not a requirement of the evolutionary Plan to go without sleep, it is also not necessary to go without continual fresh starts. This activity of reincarnation provides opportunities for purifying consciousness on the lower plane so that it can rise to the higher planes of activity.

In *The Secret Triangle* the law of rebirth is the COVENANT that God made with humanity in the story of Noah and the Ark. It promises progressive development from gross material form to a spiritual form of perfection. Its law of return along with cause and effect is called Karma and accounts for differences in personality and circumstances in life. Every soul experiences conditions that will benefit and expand consciousness of Reality.

It is not uncommon to feel that you have been with certain individuals in past lives. That is because we incarnate in groups, through cycles, and continue to learn through relationships to practice wisdom and love. Eventually, we become conscious of our group and work for the good of that group as we all are learning together. The more interested the soul is in serving the group on the material physical plane the faster it will reincarnate after death. Rebirth will continue until the soul no longer has desire for objective outer existence but identifies with substance on the higher planes. Some souls evolve rapidly; some take eons to cycle through the system.

VIBRATIONAL FREQUENCIES

The Physics of the Creation Story of Genesis shows us that everything is vibrating energy of which there are three kinds:

- Radiant energy that travels as electromagnetic waves.
- Luminous energy in the form of visible light
- Potential energy that is stored according to the relative position of various parts of a system. i.e. a steel ball has more energy above ground than after it falls to the earth.

Energy acts to bind, to conserve and to absorb. It acts in duality. It acts as high energy (accelerated motion). It acts as Kenetic (motion). It acts as a constant (as in quantum stable electrons), and it is an activator to make stable electrons active. I ask you now to review this and think of these kinds of energy being our material body. Matter is the elementary substance of the universe. Is not our physical body made of matter? Is it not equipped with all the action needed to change it into a body of light? Matter and energy are really different forms of the same thing. Each can be turned into the other. The energy defined as radiance that travels in the form of electromagnetic waves, is also luminous, and can be seen in the form of visible radiation. Is not this visible radiance the same as matter?

Why is it turned into radiating light? The answer is because of vibration, which is the periodic motion of movement in opposing directions from a position of equilibrium that has been disturbed.

This produces frequencies of vibration. These frequencies produce alternating current, and sound according to the number of complete oscillations per second. It also produces electromagnetic radiation. The velocity, or rate of motion, depends upon individual consciousness. The higher the vibration, the greater is the speed of motion. When Truth of Being is understood the vibratory rate of the body is stepped up to a high frequency that allows for ascension of the body.

This can occur when the thought and feeling (head and heart) are united into the awareness of a Spiritual Identity.

Glossary

Archetype: A perfected pattern or potential on the higher plane for the individual soul and humanity as a whole evolving on the lower planes in the present cycle. When the evolution is complete, the potential is actualized and the souls are perfected.

Astral Plane: Sphere of nature between the physical plane and the mental plane. This plane of desires is a field of sensations, passions, and instincts of the lower nature. Here are also patterns and forms that are the result of mental action on the mental plane.

Battle: Conflict between mental and emotional aspects of the soul that are spiritually energized. Every struggle is a battle against ignorant fear, the conquering of which brings wisdom and love, therefore every battle is God's battle. These are symbolized in the Bible as the battles Israelites fought.

Christ: The Cosmic Higher Self and Archetypal form or pattern principle produced from the Absolute. This Cosmic Son (sun of radiant energy) enters into experience through sacrifice and is thereby temporarily limited as individualized Christs. The Christ is also in everything, all forms, even those other than human. Each has the potential of their full expression as the Plan of reciprocal action and return is accomplished.

Consciousness: The whole of the Absolute on the mental plane, or in Mind, which is immortal, eternal, perfect. In manifestation consciousness becomes dual and is in apparent conflict but is actually mutually helpful to the seemingly opposite so that the supremacy of the Higher Self may occur. This supremacy will be the reign of the Christ as the result of union between higher and lower planes of mental activity and between the Higher Self and the lower self.

Cosmic Plane: The Archetypal Form universe that underlies the outer spiritual universe or pattern of the mental, astral, and physical universes which are the microcosms of the macrocosm and the fiery central energy Source of the system. This Comic Plane is the first aspect of the creative system out of which will follow the Solar aspect and the Planetary aspect, making up the three aspects of the system.

Days: The inhalation and then the releasing of the Divine Breath set up cycles that are periods of activity on the upper planes, thus producing involution or involvement of Spirit in matter.

Death: A belief in human consciousness that there is a limit to life. It is a belief in the absence of Life, an illusion, since God is always present and eternal. A release from the lower level of consciousness to the higher mental causal level where the soul rests until drawn once again into incarnation on the lower material plane.

Electricity: A form of energy manifested by the action of electrons and protons, minute particles bearing electrical attraction. Electricity can be generated by friction, by chemical action (battery) or by motion of a conductor in a magnetic field (dynamo).

Electron: Basic unit of negative electricity which associates with a positively charged nucleus to form the atom. The physical and chemical properties of matter are determined by the action and grouping of electrons.

Esoteric: Intelligible to a few, abstruse, taught only to a select few, not obvious.

Etheric body: A fluidic network that serves as a structural pattern upon which the material body is built and which sustains that physical body.

Ethers: An all-pervading fluid which serves to transmit heat and light waves.

Evolution: Growth, development from simple forms to more complex forms biologically; also, growth development from simplicity to complexities of consciousness outside space-time. The gradual ascent of Spirit energy from dense matter to liberation of Spirit from matter.

Evil: Belief in separation from good. It is Fear. A condition of consciousness that is imbalanced in its development of the soul qualities. The ignorance of the "sleepy" state in which the soul is immersed in its descent into form. It is an emptiness seeking to be filled and implies the absence of completeness during the process of evolution. This is only temporary. It is living backwards (EVIL—LIVE) from a perspective that is not Reality.

Exoteric: Easily understood, not secret or private, evident, opposite of esoteric.

Hologram: An interference pattern of light waves cast through a series of mirrors and a lens onto a photographic plate which produces a "seeming" three dimensional object. Interference is produced by splitting a laser beam in two different directions, through mirrors and lenses in order to produce two frequencies of vibration that interfere with each other. This produces waves that can interact and thus reproduce a form in mid air.

Involution: Process of Life and Substance descending into matter and taking on form. The Divine, "only begotten living soul" acts as a Spiritual "germ" as it descends to the lower mental and emotional planes. There it becomes the progenitor of evolution through a myriad of human souls.

Logos: The WORD, or utterance of the One Creative Energy. The Breath of Speech or of the Divine pouring out of Itself on the upper planes to make forms and then descending to the lower planes for the same purpose. All forms are the visible image produced through sound, words, breath; all the vibrating movement of God energy.

Planetary Plane: The third aspect of the system wherein electricity is the force of energy active in all forms which have manifested out of the

Light of the Solar Plane. The level of greatest density in manifestation, which is undergoing a process of purification and transformation.

Physics: A science dealing with the laws and properties of matter.

Quantum: Basic unit of energy emitted in a single wave motion of radiation.

Reincarnation: Successive embodiments of the individualized soul to enable it to gain experience, so that it can ultimately transform lower matter into spiritual essence. It provides opportunity for unfoldment of latent spiritual qualities.

Religion: Science of the spiritual life and knowledge of the process of soul growth from imperfection to perfection, from ignorance to wisdom, from separateness to love, from illusion to Truth. The popular religions of the world are states of thought and emotions produced from a belief in certain scriptures and myths, mostly viewed from the literal standpoint and misunderstood. These religions have taken form according to their particular culture and social structure so as to transform the personal nature into the impersonal. Although incomprehensible, their doctrines do serve to stimulate speculative and self-reflective thought.

Scripture, Sacred: Ancient writings of all religions which profess to be of Divine origin and to be correct transcriptions of communications received into the minds of selected persons, who faithfully have set them down.

Solar Plane: The product of the Original Cosmic Plane Energy and the second aspect of the system. It manifests as a polarity principle and is the initiation of universal sex (the opposites seeking union). This Plane of Light Intelligence expresses through principle as it extend its Light, heat, sound and vibration.

Soul: The embodiment of consciousness of the eternal Christ Self. From the One comes the many. This Christ Self identity descends and is adorned with unique qualities by raising itself through right action. The outpouring of universal Divine Love until perfect harmony with the Christ consciousness is established. While experiencing through human evolution, the soul operates through three aspects of mind; the sub-conscious, the conscious, and the Super-consciousness.

Spirit: Positive, energetic, forceful, formative movement of the Divine outpouring of energy. The passive, original life principle is of itself "soulless," without consciousness of independent "I AM," but when it is set into motion, it is "ensouled" as "I AM," thus allowing for experience of life on all levels of Mind.

Wave: A vibratory motion of regular frequency.

About the Author

Rebecca Lynne had a "wake up call" when she was in her late thirties. As a result, she began years of study and was licensed as a Metaphysical Teacher in the Unity Movement in 1975. In 1979 she received Ordination from the Association of Unity Churches. She served as an effective Counselor, Teacher, and Minister in the Unity Movement until retiring. Known for her exceptional metaphysical insight of the Bible, The Ancient Mysteries, worldwide Religions and Philosophies, she has continued to teach and share new realizations by traveling to Unity Churches to speak and present Workshops. She acts as a bridge to those who are dissatisfied with traditional theology and want a spiritual teaching that has no particular creed and dogma. Lynne's theology breaks through the confines of old forms and embraces all religions because it enters into the abstract realm of ideas that demand a correlation of Religion, Science and Philosophy. Her emphasis is upon Universal Laws that act the same way whether in the material realm or in the spiritual realms of the Infinite Universal Mind. She presents a unity between Science and Religion.

Although now in her eighties, Rebecca Lynne is still teaching and learning by sharing Truth. Humanity is "waking up" with more speed than ever before.

You are welcome to contact Rebecca with comments or questions about this book through this link Innervoice@ GenesisPhysics.com.